THE AMERICAN GAME

ALSO BY IRA ROSEN

Blue Skies, Green Fields

THE AMERICAN GAME

A CELEBRATION OF MINOR LEAGUE BASEBALL

IRA ROSEN

Collins

An Imprint of HarperCollinsPublishers

FIRST EDITION

Designed by William Ruoto

Library of Congress Cataloging-in-Publication Data is available.

ISBN-10 0-06-089779-1
ISBN-13 978-0-06-089779-6

06 07 08 09 10 RRD 10 9 8 7 6 5 4 3 2 1

For Deborah Peckham,
and for the fans,
who make baseball what it is.

**"I see great things in baseball.
It's our game—the American game."**

Walt Whitman, poet (1819–1892)

Acknowledgments

SPECIAL THANKS TO my wife, Judy, for the creative, logistical, editorial, and emotional support.

Thanks to: Deborah Peckham, my attorney—my advocate—who stepped up to the plate.

Knox Huston, my editor, and Joe Tessitore, at Collins, for believing in my work, and for being baseball fans. And Matthew Benjamin, for seeing it through.

John Beneway, for my Web site design and tech support.

Arline Beneway-Lugert, the world's greatest mother-in-law.

The Beneway and the McLaughlin families for the encouragement.

Chuck Bernice, for the business advice and friendship.

Denise Wood and the Wood Family, for their hospitality.

John Castronovo at TPI, Fairfield, NJ, for the digital scans.

Steve Krintzman at Technicraft, for the commiseration.

All of the folks in media relations and front offices at the Major League and Minor League ballparks for extending me professional courtesy.

Everyone who shared minor league experiences with me.

Again, to coach Anthony Lagos who, a long time ago, told me to "keep working at it."

And Dr. Larry (Mets Employee Assistance) who reminded me that I have a choice.

Contents

Introduction

THE GAME OF BASEBALL is still America's pastime. From Little League to the major leagues, there is no sport that combines its leisurely, timeless pace with its most difficult challenge—hitting a thrown ball. Millions of kids try to master the art and science of playing the game well enough to eventually make a living at it. Very few do. For every thousand high school players, only one will sign a professional contract. And of those, only two will ever wear a major league uniform. The rest will toil in the minor leagues, riding buses for up to eighteen hours at a time and in some cases earning less than minimum wage.

Mention baseball to folks and most think of millionaire players and billionaire owners—the big leagues. More fans attend major league games (75 million in 2005) than minor league games (more than 41 million in 2005). But in August 1994, the Major League Baseball players went on strike. No one knew it would happen, but several weeks later, the season was lost and the World Series canceled. To fill the void in that baseball summer, millions of fans attended minor league games, many for the first time. It was the beginning of the growth that resulted in the current all-time high popularity level of Minor League Baseball.

My wife and I were among those fans, setting out to visit the National Baseball Hall of Fame in Cooperstown, New York, and to catch a few ball games along the way. Our first stop that year was in Colonie, New York, at the time the home of the Double-A Albany Yankees. With the team just two stops from the majors, the game was an opportunity to see good professional baseball up close. It was also a chance to see a highly touted prospect I was vaguely aware of, a shortstop named Derek Jeter.

Entering a minor league ballpark is not quite the same thing as walking up the ramp in a big-league stadium. There are fewer fans, so the structures are smaller. The ballplayers aren't as famous, so there is less security. Of course, these are positives, considering the proximity to the playing field of virtually every seat, and the access to the ballplayers for the fans, especially youngsters. Talking with a ballplayer in uniform, or even getting an autograph of a major leaguer is very difficult these days. Not so in the minors. A great part of the fun I observed that day was dozens of kids talking to and receiving autographs from nearly every Albany Yankee player. Once the game started, I noted that most of the crowd was young: babies and children with parents, teenagers socializing. The feeling was entirely different from the businesslike atmosphere at most big-league stadiums. It was very gratifying to us to see the next generation of baseball fans having a great time.

As the game wore on, my attention turned to watching Jeter at bat and in the field. It was obvious why he was so highly regarded. Running to his left toward a ground ball hit up the middle, he appeared gangly but coltlike, with impressive agility. Ranging deep into the hole, he made the shortstop's most difficult throw easily, with velocity and accuracy. During his first at bat, with the count 2-0, the pitcher threw a changeup—a common pitch selection at the big-league level, uncommon in Double-A. Jeter, with a wide stance and hands held high, stayed back and lined the ball sharply up the middle, showing patience and bat speed. These images remain in my mind's eye; it was a special moment, seeing a teenage prospect who would eventually mature into a four-time world champion and potential Hall of Famer.

Next stop: Binghamton. I caught the future double-play combo for the New York Mets, Edgardo Alfonzo and Rey Ordonez. I also saw players at the ballpark who did not become successful. Playing first base for the Binghamton Mets was Frank Jacobs, a big, handsome former football star at Notre Dame. Approaching a Mets scout seated behind home plate, I asked him about Jacobs. He replied, "He's only a Double-A player." And he was right—Jacobs never made the majors. I also watched a pitchers' duel between Juan Acevedo, at the time a Colorado Rockies prospect, and Bill Pulsipher of the B-Mets. Sitting in the first row behind home plate, I thought Acevedo had better stuff and much better mechanics. Unfortunately, Pulsipher blew out his elbow a couple of years later and has never fulfilled his potential.

Since then, I have attended more minor league than major league games, and I still enjoy trying to pick out the players that I think might make "the Show" someday, as well as those that I think won't.

There are many more wonderful facets of Minor League Baseball: some of the best and most reasonably priced ballpark food—the strawberry ice cream and fresh hot pretzels at MacArthur Stadium in Syracuse, New York; the Zweigle's Red Hots at Silver Stadium in Rochester, New York. These rickety old ballparks have since been replaced, but the fans who attended games there will always remember them. Additionally, the between-innings activities reflect the unique zaniness that epitomizes the minor leagues: dizzy bat races, water balloon tosses, and the ever-popular "What's in the Box?", a contest I witnessed for the first time at Frontier Field in Rochester, New York ("How should *I* know what's in the box??!?" "Oh, you just *pick* one and *win what's in it* . . .").

While conducting interviews for this book, I discovered that many minor league players love baseball as much as the fans do. Although most of them are playing to reach the big leagues, some play simply because they crave the competition and camaraderie. Their stories both cheered me, as I saw my own struggles reflected in their determination, and saddened me, since a lot of the players I spoke with will never realize their dreams. There is magic in baseball—and a lot of it happens here.

Author's Notes: The facts and figures listed for the ballparks are as of April, 2006, and are for informational purposes only. While I strove for accuracy, some sources provided conflicting data.

All photographs © Ira Rosen / Stadium Views, Inc.

A portion of the proceeds from this book will be donated to the Baseball Assistance Team (BAT).

PART ONE

THE MINOR LEAGUES

Each section of *The American Game* focuses on a specific classification of professional baseball. This first section is an overview of the experience of the entire minor leagues, and consists of old ballparks from various levels. While I was compiling material for this book, a number of ballparks were replaced by newer ones. Similar to old major league stadiums, some of these older facilities remain standing, serving their communities in different ways. Others have been demolished. In every case, the lost ballparks—large or small, good or bad—hold fond memories for millions of fans, and I believe that this is an appropriate way of honoring these green fields.

Donovan Stadium

DONOVAN STADIUM

- ◆ Former Home of the Utica Blue Sox
  (New York–Penn League, Single-A—1981–2001)

- ◆ Former Home of the Utica Blue Jays
  (New York–Penn League, Single-A—1977–1980)

- ◆ Location—170 Sunset Avenue, Utica, New York

- ◆ Opened—1977

- ◆ Seating Capacity—4,000

- ◆ LF 324 CF 390 RF 324

Donovan Stadium at Murnane Field is the official name. Among the ballplayers who played here are Larry Walker, Ray Durham, James Baldwin, and Mike Cameron.

DAVE NELSON (Former Major League Player; Major League Coach) "I signed a professional baseball contract in 1964 with the Cleveland Indians. I grew up in Los Angeles with some great players: Reggie Smith, Roy White, the late Don Wilson, Bobby Tolan, Willie Crawford, Bob Watson, and Charlie Murray, Eddie Murray's brother. Eddie was our batboy on the sandlot team we all played on. The Indians sent me to Dubuque, Iowa. It was something that I wasn't ready for. There were five black players on the team. They put us up at the YMCA, which was an old building. They had apartments for the white players. A lot of the restaurants wouldn't serve us. Security guards would follow you, thinking you're going to steal something. I told my mom that I was quitting because baseball wasn't what I thought it was. She said, 'Who's your idol?' I said, 'Jackie Robinson.' She asked, 'Are you going

Ira Rosen

through what he went through?' I said, 'Well, no.' She said, 'Then what's the problem? You're going to let these people destroy your dream? Destroy what Jackie's worked for all these years, to go through what he went through to make it possible for you to play? You'll find a way to overcome it and survive.' And I did. If it wasn't for Jackie and my mom, I wouldn't be here today."

TOM GLAVINE (Major League Pitcher) "The minor leagues is your starting point. The beginning of a dream. [It's] the uncertainty of it all, but at the same time feeling you're getting an opportunity to at least chase a dream. Each step along the way, the improvements you have to make to get to the next level. The competition, the grind every year. You just didn't know what was going to happen."

MIKE CAMERON (Major League Player) "The bonds that you form. I've got many close friendships because of this game—James Baldwin, just talked to him a few days ago. The things you learn, the things that got you here. I try to remember those things, especially when I put on a big-league uniform every day."

MIKE BERTOTTI (Former Major League Pitcher) "I played in Scottsdale in the Arizona Fall League in '94. I was fortunate enough to play with Michael Jordan, with Birmingham and Scottsdale. A good friend of mine, my locker mate in Birmingham. After our day game in Scottsdale on a Sunday afternoon, a bunch of guys on the team would get together at a local park, play a little pickup hoops. I was fortunate enough when we played a five-on-five game, shot a three-pointer over him. I thought he was playing good defense at the time, he was taking it kind of serious. So I kinda got in his mug a little bit, said, 'Mike, I thought you got Defensive Player of the Year, you're letting a 6'1" white guy shoot a three-pointer over you.' He goes, 'Yeah, well, why don't you try guarding me?' I was as serious as I could possibly be, him taking the ball down the court next time, giving my best defensive impersonation.

Mike Cameron, New York Mets, Petco Park, 2004

The biggest thing was him looking in my eyes, going, 'Are you ready, are you ready?' I go, 'Yeah I'm ready.' And in one quick move he was gone. One dribble, he's by me, laying it up into the hoop. I've never seen anything like that. It's something that I can share with my kids someday."

NATE ESPY (Minor League Player) "The best thing is the camaraderie. You become so close during the season with all you go through. All you have is your teammates; everybody trying to reach that goal, the sacrifices you go through together. It's just total respect for one another. It's like a family."

ROD NICHOLS (Minor League Coach) "Minor League Baseball is chasing the dream. Not necessarily myself as a coach chasing a dream, but helping the players. It's hard work, there's no money, long bus rides."

6   Ira Rosen

RICARDO JORDAN (Former Major League Pitcher) "My favorite thing about Minor League Baseball is you come to know the fans. I've met some fans that I still keep in touch with. In the big leagues, the players don't really get involved with the fans.

TIM THOMPSON (Scout) "I started scouting in 1963 with the Dodgers. I replaced Tom Lasorda in the eastern part of the United States. I was only there one year. Mr. Campanis told me they weren't going to scout in the East anymore. I went to work for the Cardinals about two weeks after he let me go. I spent thirty years with the Cardinals. I had seven states. Signed Brian Jordan, John Mabry, Tommy Herr. Altogether, signed nine or ten big-league players. With the draft, it eliminates a lot of things in scouting. You knew all about the families, the kids. Without the draft, it was more fun."

Durham Athletic Park

DURHAM ATHLETIC PARK

- *Former Home of the Durham Bulls (Piedmont League, Single-A—1926–1943; Carolina League, Single-A—1945–1971, 1980–1994)*

- *Location—Washington Street, Durham, North Carolina*

- *Opened—1926 as El Toro Park; renamed Durham Athletic Park, 1933*

- *Destroyed June 17, 1939; rebuilt July 2, 1939*

- *Last Professional Game—June 5, 1994*

- *Seating Capacity—5,000*

- *LF 330 CF 410 RF 307*

"The Dap" was the site of the filming of the 1988 feature film Bull Durham. *The ballpark is no longer used for minor league games, but is still in use for local ballgames and community events. Among the ballplayers who played here are Chipper Jones, Joe Morgan, Ryan Klesko, and David Justice.*

Durham Bulls Baseball Club, Inc.

GOOD THIS
DATE ONLY
FRIDAY
SEPT.
3
1993
NO REFUND

Admit One
Durham Bulls
vs. Kinston

FAREWELL SEASON
AT THE DAP

Price $6.00

SEC.BX
TKT. NO.
RESERVED SEAT
479

RAIN CHECK

10 Ira Rosen

BOB BOONE (Former Major League Player; Former Major League Manager) "I have a lot of good memories from playing in Durham when it was A-ball. Watching the movie *Bull Durham* and going, 'Yeah, I think that's there.' In the minor leagues, you're much closer with all of the people. When you don't have any money, you have to make your fun by having friends, doing things with them. The wives were much closer."

STEVE BLASS (Former Major League Pitcher; Broadcaster) "Susan Sarandon was not in the Carolina League when I was there or I would still be there!"

RYAN KLESKO (Major League Player) "My first year in pro ball, I was doing pretty well. I hated where we were at—it was hot and humid. I wasn't used to that—I'm from Southern California. We had bunk beds, no TVs, and phone booths downstairs. No air conditioning on the buses. I went up to one of my coaches and said, 'I don't know if I made the right decision. This sucks. What do I need to do to get out of here?' He looked at me and said, 'Hit.' I proceeded to hit about .400. I went four-for-four one day. My last at bat, they went to intentionally walk me. [The pitcher] left the ball too close to the plate. I slapped it for a hit to win the game. My coach said, 'Good job. By the way, go carry the equipment in.' I was a little mad—I just went five-for-five, won the game, and the guy's making me carry in equipment. He said, 'This is your last day here, you got called up.' "

REGGIE JACKSON (Hall of Fame Player) "It's a great place for enthusiasm. The game is pure, the players are pure. The fans see really good, pure baseball. You get to see players that one day could become stars in the big leagues."

BILLY WILLIAMS (Hall of Fame Player) "When you first sign to play professional baseball, your first coach always leaves a lasting memory. Mine was Don Bieble, when I had him in Ponca City, Oklahoma, down in the Sooner State League in 1956. I was one of those guys that 'filled the roster.' Because Lou Johnson had gotten his ear cut off, he was in the hospital. So I made the roster but didn't go on any road trips. When the team went on the road, they would give me two and a quarter days' meal money, so I stayed around Ponca City. Saw a lot of rodeos in Oklahoma. Didn't get a chance to play that much that year. Second year, 1957, I played in 130 games. I was a skinny kid, weighed 155 pounds. We had four guys on that Class D team make it to the major leagues: Jim Brewer, Lou Johnson, Sammy Drake, and myself."

MIKE BORDICK (Former Major League Player) "When I was a young player, I was really naive about the whole situation. When I got to my first year in short season, I thought that was the best place to be. I think everybody's hopes are that you get the opportunity to be in the big leagues the next year.

Ryan Klesko, San Diego Padres, Petco Park, 2004

Next year I went to Single-A, and I thought that was the best place to be. My naïveté helped me to not get too far ahead of myself. I was able to stay at each level for a full year and learn. When I finally made it to the big leagues, I realized the big leagues is the only place to play."

DOUG GLANVILLE (Former Major League Player) "It's a long road. I remember fifteen-hour bus rides from Orlando to Memphis, and playing a full season in Double-A without a day off because we were always traveling. That was 140 games. I ran across a lot of amazing people. Jimmy Piersall was an outfield

Ira Rosen

coach. He was an incredible coach and insane at the same time. He always stayed with me and was a great supporter. Tom Gamboa was my coach in Puerto Rico. He really gave me a great opportunity when I played winter ball to really relax and play my game. It springboarded my career to the next level. I played in Des Moines, Iowa—I never thought I'd live there in my life. In Geneva, New York, in the New York–Penn League, the sun set in left-center field—you couldn't see the first four innings."

ED LYNCH (Former Major League Pitcher and Executive; Broadcaster) "The minors are really the pure essence of baseball; there is really not the financial or media pressure on these kids. They still play the game for a lot of the right reasons. The fans have a lot of intimate contact. It's a lot of fun for kids; there are a lot of promotions between innings. It's just a different atmosphere. You've got the best players in the world at the major league level, but down at the minor league level it's a fun, family atmosphere. I think Brooklyn is one of the best I've ever seen.

You really don't understand the function of the minor leagues when you're a player; you're just trying to work your way to the big leagues. It's really your research and development department. You have to be very patient with it. When you're a player, you don't understand that patience. When you're developing players, you have to make sure you bring them along in a timely manner. You don't rush them; you try to push them so that they're challenged but not to the point where they don't have a reasonable chance of success."

MacArthur Stadium

MacArthur Stadium

- *Former Home of the Syracuse Chiefs (International League, Triple-A, 1961–1996)*
- *Location—East Hiawatha Boulevard, Syracuse, New York*
- *Opened—1934*
- *Cost—$255,000*
- *Refurbished—1988*
- *Final Game—September 3, 1996*
- *Seating Capacity—10,500*
- *LF 320 CF 434 RF 320*

Formerly named Municipal Stadium (1934–1941), MacArthur Stadium was replaced by P & C Stadium (now named Alliance Bank Stadium) in 1997. Among the ballplayers who played there were Carlos Delgado, Shawn Green, and Ron Guidry.

Ira Rosen

ERIC VALENT (Minor League Player) "I was a first-round draft choice, supplemental pick out of UCLA in 1998. Played full-season A-Ball in 1999, was an all-star. The next year, I played Double-A, I was an all-star. Then I was put on the major league roster. For the next two years, it was Triple-A, big leagues, Triple-A, big leagues. This is the first year I've been able to break with a team from opening day. It's not that it's been a struggle, it's that you run into a lot of competition. I do a lot of things well, but I'm not a superstar. It might take me a little bit longer. When you're put on a major league roster, they have three options on you, which means they can send you to the minor leagues as many times as they want for three years. Now I'm out of those—hopefully I can keep competing and stay."

CARLOS DELGADO (Major League Player) "My favorite memory is the end of the season in 1994. Major League Baseball went on strike, and we had a very good team in Triple-A. I remember we went to the finals against the Richmond Braves. We had Alex Gonzalez, Shawn Green. That was a good time. For myself, it was tough because I went to the big leagues first, then went back to the minor leagues, so you get spoiled in the big leagues. When I got to MacArthur Stadium, I said, 'You know what, I want to get out of here!' In the big leagues, you have to be patient, stay consistent. I got in trouble when I was a little impatient. Once you learn that—it comes with experience—you've got a better idea of what you can do, when to be aggressive, when to be patient. That makes the difference."

DAVE MAGADAN (Former Major League Player; Major League Coach) "I was having trouble with my footwork at first base. [At] my first Instructional League, Mike Cubbage gave me a jump rope. He told me to learn how—I had never jumped rope before. It was a godsend—it was amazing how much it helped. When I went over to third base, Sam Perlozzo did a drill with me where he got about twenty-five to thirty feet away from me, and hit balls as hard as he could right at me. I'd be

Carlos Delgado, Syracuse Cheifs, MacArthur Stadium, 1994

Shannon Stewart, Toronto Blue Jays, Great American Ballpark, 2003

up against the backstop. He really worked with me on one-step quickness. I didn't become Brooks Robinson, but I became good enough to play third base in the big leagues."

SAL RENDE (Minor League Coach) "I started as a player in 1977. I led the New York–Penn League in hitting one year. [But] I quit playing when I was twenty-seven. That pretty much speaks for itself. I started managing in A-ball in 1984. I've been coaching since then. I've had no experience in the major leagues. If it happens, it happens. My life is not dependent on whether I make it to the big leagues or not. I'm driven to get there because it's a better place to be as far as benefits. I have a wife and two boys. It's a hard lifestyle. I haven't been together with my family [yet] this summer. I go from the middle of February, and for the most part, I might see them for a home stand or a road trip somewhere during the course of the year. So it's six, seven months away from your family every year. That's the one drawback about being in baseball."

SHANNON STEWART (Major League Player) "There was one guy that helped me out and made me the hitter I am today: Larry Hisle, ex-ballplayer, Milwaukee Brewers. I developed a good relationship with this gentleman. He taught me how to hit, but he also taught me things about life, being a person. I still keep in touch with him. He had a very big influence in my career."

HARMON KILLEBREW (Hall of Fame Player) "Playing in the minor leagues is a necessary thing you have to do. I was a young kid when I came up to the major leagues, only seventeen years old. There are so many things you can only learn by playing every day. It took me going to the minor leagues in order to learn those things.

"[In 1958] I was with the Washington Senators for about a month. They said they were sending me to the minors—they didn't have a Triple-A team in those days, so they sent me to Indianapolis, which was a White Sox farm club. I was there about a month. It took me a while to get going, because that was really a good league. I was just starting to hit the ball and they said, 'We're sending you back to Chattanooga.' That was kind of a crossroads in my career. I had to make a decision as to what to do. I did go back and finished the year there, did very well. Went back at the end of the year to Washington, stayed, and the next year I played my first year as a regular for the Senators in 1959."

Silver Stadium

SILVER STADIUM

- ◆ Former Home of the Rochester Red Wings
  (International League, Triple-A)
- ◆ Location—500 Norton Street, Rochester, New York
- ◆ Opening Day—May 2, 1929
- ◆ Largest Crowd—19,006 (May 5, 1931)
- ◆ Refurbished—1986
- ◆ Cost—$4.5 million
- ◆ Final Game—August 30, 1996
- ◆ Seating Capacity—11,500
- ◆ LF 320 CF 415 RF 315

Originally named Red Wing Stadium, Silver Stadium was replaced by Frontier Field in 1997. Among the ballplayers who played there were Cal Ripken, Stan Musial, and Bob Gibson.

Ira Rosen

MARTY BRENNAMAN (Hall of Fame Broadcaster) "[In the minor leagues] I worked only at the Triple-A level, so I was blessed, I guess. We flew everywhere. I did the Tidewater [Tides] games, which is now Norfolk. I did those games in 1971, 1972, and 1973. I worked in a league with players who went on to become outstanding big-league players: Don Baylor at Rochester, Bobby Grich, Jim Bibby. I especially liked Silver Stadium in Rochester, which is no longer there. Silver was one of the all-time great minor league ballparks. I know it reached the point where it was way past antiquated when they finally had to take it down. I liked MacArthur in Syracuse. It was a Yankee Triple-A farm club then. I wouldn't trade the experience of having worked in Minor League Baseball."

JIM RUSHFORD (Former Major League Player) "I played four years at San Diego State. I went undrafted. I pitched and hit. Took a year off and worked. Played Independent ball for a year. Did well, had a great time. Went to all sorts of tryout camps, trying to get picked up. Wasn't. Played for the Mission Viejo Vigilantes in the Western League. Pitched about seven innings, got lit up. Got released. After being released from Independent ball, I figured I had no more options left. Worked for two years at odd jobs: personal trainer, bouncer, roofer, pizza deliveryman, moving company—by far the worst job. Played semipro ball. Following year, I tried out for an Independent team again, the Schaumberg Flyers in the Northern League. I started doing well, getting a chance to play every day as a hitter. Halfway through the season I ran into an outfield wall, fractured a rib and separated a shoulder. That was going to be my last hurrah, but I kind of felt cheated, so I went back for another year. [But] they traded me to Duluth, and that's when I had a breakout season, in 2000. A manager I had, R. C. Lichtenstein, helped me get signed with the Milwaukee Brewers. I played A-ball and Double-A as a twenty-seven-year old. Following year I played Triple-A and got a big-league call-up in 2002. Got about a month of playing time. In 2003 I started with the Texas Rangers.

Jim Rushford, Scranton/Wilkes-Barre Red Barons, Lackawanna County Stadium, 2004

Had a bad first month in Triple-A and was released. The Brewers picked me back up and I did well, but didn't get any more big-league time. The Phillies signed me for 2004.

"I have a wife and two kids. It's just as difficult for them. They're put out a lot by all the traveling and moving. My wife—at times it's like being a single mom for her. The uncertainty—your career can end any day. You don't even get two weeks' notice. You just walk in one day and they tell you you're released—no paycheck, no insurance, no nothing. There's zero security. Other than the guys who get million-dollar signing bonuses, everyone else has to worry every day. But just to play baseball every day is enough to make it all worth it.

"I went back to San Diego State this past off-season to work with Tony Gwynn. I wear number nineteen because of all the time he dedicated to me."

MATT GINTER (Minor League Pitcher) "I played at Mississippi State. My two roommates were Travis Chapman [played with the Phillies] and Jon Knott, who's with San Diego. Our whole house has made it to the big leagues, which I think is pretty amazing. I was the twenty-second pick in the first round to the White Sox in 1999. They sent me to Arizona at first, then to Burlington, Iowa. More or less like *Bull Durham*—small stadium, bad fields. We ended up winning the Midwest League. Our record was 71–68. I've been around a lot of guys who've never won any kind of championship at any level. Even though it was A-ball, you got a ring. Got a little 'B' on top of it.

"Next year, I went to Double-A in Birmingham. Our starting rotation was me, Mark Buehrle, Josh Fogg, Rocky Biddle, and Jon Rauch. Me and Rauch made the 2000 Olympics team. They did not let me go because I got called up to the big leagues. First day, I came into a game in the eighth inning, down six runs. I go one-two-three. We scored seven runs in the bottom of the eighth inning. I shut the door, got the win. First day in the big leagues."

PAT STRANGE (Minor League Pitcher) "I was a high school draft pick, so I knew I had at least a few years in the minor leagues to become a seasoned player and try to get to the major leagues. I had an older brother who played professional baseball, so I had a heads-up on what was going to happen. It's been pretty much what I expected—a lot of travel, a lot of homesickness, a lot of small towns. And I wouldn't trade it for anything. It doesn't get any better, until you get to the major leagues. I was up and down the last couple of years. [I'm working on] discipline and mound command. I think all my pitches are there, the talent is there, I just need to get focused and work on being consistent enough to start in the major leagues."

ED FARMER (Former Major League Pitcher; Broadcaster) "I came to the big leagues quick. There really wasn't an adjustment. I played Rookie ball my first year when I was seventeen, then broke camp with the big-league team the next year. I came up as a starter, then they put me in the bullpen. They needed a guy to throw hard and get ten or twelve outs. But they sent me down to Waterbury, then to Reno, where all my friends were. The following year I was in the big leagues again. I was nineteen, I didn't know what I was doing."

War Memorial Stadium

WAR MEMORIAL STADIUM

- *Former Home of the Greensboro Bats
  (South Atlantic League, Single-A)*

- *Location—Bennett Avenue and Lindsay Street, Greensboro, North
  Carolina*

- *Opened—1926*

- *Seating Capacity—7,500*

- *LF 327 CF 401 RF 327*

*War Memorial Stadium was replaced by First Horizon Park in 2005.
Among the ballplayers who played there were Derek Jeter, Mariano Rivera,
and Don Mattingly.*

1993 GREENSBORO HORNETS

It's a Whole New Ballgame...
in the Country's Oldest
Minor League Park!

Catch all 143 games on
1320 AM

Ira Rosen

JOHN BURKETT (Former Major League Pitcher) "Whenever you have failure, you're going to have doubt. Even if you make it to the major leagues. The difference is being able to get through that, figuring it out, being able to succeed even though you feel that doubt. Being able to grab onto something positive and run with it. Being in the minor leagues was tough for me, especially the first couple of years. I didn't pitch all that well, but I got with a pitching coach named Marty DeMeritt. I had him from 1985 to 1990. He was a big help for me. He taught me how to pitch in the big leagues. He got me to where I am today."

HOWARD JOHNSON (Former Major League Player; Minor League Coach) "My favorite part of managing in the minor leagues is when you get a chance to send a kid up to a higher level. That's what they want, that's what we want. My least favorite part—bus rides, without a doubt. Anything over three or four hours, forget about it. I hate it; that and sending a guy down or releasing a player. Those are the hardest things. When they come into pro ball, they

have a burning desire to get to the big leagues. When you've got to tell them that they can't do that anymore, that's tough."

DEREK JETER (Major League Player) "One of the biggest jumps is to go from Single-A to Double-A. I think getting called up then was pretty special because it came halfway through the season. The biggest adjustment was probably the pitchers. They throw more strikes with their off-speed pitches. I think in the lower levels, pitchers have a tough time controlling off-speed pitches. As you move up they get more control."

BILL DANCY (Major League Coach) "The minor league experience has been a challenge from when I signed in 1973 all the way up to this point. Everybody's dream is to get to the major leagues. Some do, some don't. Unfortunately, in my situation I didn't. I was fortunate enough that the people in the Phillies organization felt strongly that I was a good baseball man and kept me in it—as a manager, as an infield coordinator, now as a field coordinator. I've benefited from all the people I've met to become a 'people person.' I would hope [my chances of getting to the big leagues] are good. But I've been around long enough to know if it happens, you have to be at the right place at the right time."

Derek Jeter, Albany Yankees, Heritage Park, 1994

Bicentennial Park

BICENTENNIAL PARK

◆ *Former Home of the Allentown Ambassadors*
   (Northern League, Eastern Division, Independent)

◆ *Location—Lehigh and South Howard Streets, Allentown, Pennsylvania*

◆ *Opened—1930*

◆ *Seating Capacity—4,600*

◆ *LF 335 CF 370 RF 310*

Officially named Earl F. Hunsicker Bicentennial Park, this ballpark is not currently in use in Minor League Baseball.

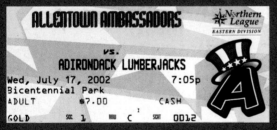

ALLENTOWN AMBASSADORS

Northern League
EASTERN DIVISION

VS.
ADIRONDACK LUMBERJACKS

Wed, July 17, 2002   7:05p
Bicentennial Park
ADULT $7.00   CASH
GOLD   SEC 1   ROW C   SEAT 0012

Ira Rosen

ED OTT (Former Major League Player; Minor League Manager) "We like to consider this stadium [Bicentennial Park] as arena baseball. It's a unique park, only 310 feet down the right field line, 394 feet to the right-center field gap. We have a fifty-foot screen in right field that is a home run. Straightaway center is probably 325 feet with a thirty-foot wall and a fifty-foot net on top of that. So that's our 'Black Monster' instead of the Green Monster up in Boston. Down the left-field line it's 330 feet and the fifty-foot net continues around. All of that net from center field to left field is in play. It's a home field advantage because you learn how to play the ball off the net. [But] it's a tough ballpark to get some pitchers to pitch for us because of the small dimensions. In Independent baseball, the guys have to put up numbers to be recognized by organizations. So it's tough to get top-notch pitchers in here because a routine fly ball to left field in normal parks is a double off the screen in our ballpark. Hitters love to hit here."

KEN GRIFFEY, JR. (Major League Player) "[The best thing was] just getting drafted, being able to play professional baseball. The biggest adjustment was wooden bats."

GREG LEGG (Former Major League Player; Minor League Manager) "I think so much of being a minor league player or manager is a lot of heart. In most cases, most of the players, coaches, and managers aren't going to make it to the big leagues. You play the game for love and character and heart in the hope that you will get to the big leagues. You don't lose sight of that dream, that I might get there or the players might get there. For me, working with the players is a lot of fun. But you know most of the time, these guys aren't going to make it. The best part is when one of those guys makes it."

WALT JOCKETTY (Major League Executive) "We're seeing that there's still a necessity for good player development, especially today with the economics of the game. I think more clubs are trying to spend more on scouting and developing their own players. In our system we have good quality pitching at the higher levels—guys like Dan Haren, Adam Wainwright, Rhett Parrott, and Jim Journell. [Good] position players in our organization are probably down at the lower level. It's fun to see how the minor leagues have evolved. I started in this game about thirty years ago in the minors. It was mostly mom-and-pop. I worked in Des Moines, Iowa, in 1975 as the assistant general manager. But you did everything back then. We were a Triple-A club—we had a three-man staff. Now even in A-ball they have eight, ten, twelve people, and even more than that at Triple-A. It's really become a big business."

Wahconah Park

WAHCONAH PARK

- Former Home of the Berkshire Black Bears
  (Northern League, Eastern Division, Independent)

- Location—North and Wahconah Streets, Pittsfield, Massachusetts

- Opened—1919

- Seating Capacity—4,000

- LF 334 CF 374 RF 333

Wahconah Park is not currently in use for Minor League Baseball. Among the ballplayers who played here are Carlton Fisk, Rafael Palmeiro, and Sparky Lyle.

2002 SEASON TICKETS

JUL 27 2002
Game 30 SAT 7:05 PM
GOOD ONLY THIS DATE
BOX SEAT

SEC	ROW	SEAT
2	A	10

BERKSHIRE BLACK BEARS

VS.

NEW JERSEY JACKALS

JUL 27 2002
SAT 7:05 PM
BOX SEAT $7.00

WAHCONAH PARK

JUL 27 2002

GAME		SAT
30		7:05 PM
2	A	10
SEC	ROW	SEAT

DALLAS GREEN (Former Major League Player and Manager; Executive) "The minor leagues are the heart and soul of baseball. I think if anybody ever forgets that, this game will be in a lot more trouble than it is. The superstars have to come from somewhere. I've watched the growth of Minor League Baseball. It's been a tremendous part of a lot of communities in the United States. I'm very proud to have been a part of it."

GEORGE GRANDE (Broadcaster) "The essence to me of the game of baseball are the people who play the game and the road that they travel to get to the major leagues. I've had a chance to follow [players] from high school, some from college. Guy that comes to mind is Mark McGwire. Saw him at USC, spent time with him, watched him when he played for Rod Dedeaux; as he went into the minor leagues, struggled; when he got to the major leagues—had a great rookie year. Called upon what he learned in the minors to get over a year where he hit barely .200. Bounced back and became one of the greatest home run hitters of all time. It goes back to the people that spend so much time and effort and energy to help them be as good as they can be. That's what this game is about."

JOSH TOWERS (Major League Pitcher) "There was a time when I was playing in the minors that I wanted to stop playing baseball. Whenever you're slumping, you question whether you're good enough to be there, or whether you're going to make it. If you're not a prospect, it's that much harder for you. As long as you don't lose sight of the dream, the goal, and stop working hard, then you shouldn't have doubts. The one time I wanted to stop playing, my mom said, 'You're going to continue to play.' I said, 'Okay.'"

TREVOR HOFFMAN (Major League Pitcher) "It's a series of ups and downs. Coming from the University of Arizona, travel was on planes to other Pac-10 cities, playing on the weekends, with a lot of hype. In Minor League Baseball, you find yourself looking out your hotel window in Butte, Montana, and wondering why the hell I'm doing this. The most fortunate thing—I went to different cities each year: Billings, Montana, to Charleston, West Virginia, to

Ira Rosen

Cedar Rapids, Iowa, to Chattanooga, Tennessee, to Nashville, Tennessee, and finally to the big leagues. I didn't have to repeat any city. The best fried chicken I've ever had was in Chattanooga, just up the street from old Engel Stadium, in a Texaco station. Next to Mom's, obviously."

Trevor Hoffman, San Diego Padres, Petco Park, 2004

PART TWO

TRIPLE-A

Triple-A is the highest level of Minor League Baseball. There are thirty teams, one for each franchise in Major League Baseball. It consists of two leagues, the International League, with fourteen teams, and the Pacific Coast League, with sixteen teams. For some ballplayers, Triple-A is the last rung on the ladder to the inevitable destination: the Show. For others, it's the first step down from the big leagues, on the way to retirement. And for the rest, Triple-A is a sort of baseball purgatory: being good enough to reach the upper levels of professional baseball while still waiting for the call that may never come.

Alliance Bank Stadium

ALLIANCE BANK STADIUM

- *Home of the Syracuse SkyChiefs (International League, Triple-A)*

- *Location—800 North Second Street, Syracuse, NY*

- *Opening Day—June 28, 1997*

- *Capacity—11,602*

- *LF 328 CF 404 RF 328*

Formerly named P & C Stadium, Alliance Bank Stadium replaced MacArthur Stadium, which was known as Municipal Stadium from 1934 to 1941. Among the ballplayers who played here are Carlos Delgado, Vernon Wells, and Chris Carpenter.

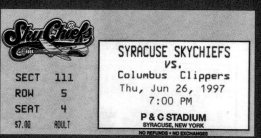

JIM LONBORG (Former Major League Pitcher) "The greatest experience I had in the minor leagues was in 1964. I started off with Winston-Salem, North Carolina, A-ball. About seven, eight weeks into the season, I was called up to Triple-A. I had some experience in college so they figured I didn't need to go to Double-A. I had the good fortune to join the Seattle Rainiers in San Diego for the first weekend, and then we got on a plane and flew to Hawaii for a week."

ANDY ETCHEBARREN (Former Major League Player; Minor League Manager) "I was in the big leagues for twenty-two years. I've had about ten years in the

Ira Rosen

minors. I really enjoy the development part. The satisfaction for me now is starting to see some of the younger players develop into prospects, which a lot of clubs in the big leagues can't do. That part's exciting, that you have twenty-two-, twenty-three-year-olds at the Triple-A level. Nowadays there are so many thirty- to thirty-five-year-olds making a good living [here]. It's completely different than when I played twenty years ago. Because if you didn't have a chance to play in the big leagues [then], you didn't play Triple-A, you went home."

GEORGE TSAMIS (Former Major League Pitcher; Minor League Manager) "One day in Triple-A I got clobbered in a game in Albuquerque. A couple of days later they called me into the office to say they're moving me to the bullpen. I had been a starter my whole career. So I got mad, told them how angry I was about it, and they said, 'Oh, by the way, you're going to Milwaukee tomorrow.' That's the day I got called up to the big leagues."

Andy Etchebarren, Rochester Red Wings, Alliance
Bank Stadium, 2001

Stu and Stan Cliburn, New Britain RockCats,
New Britain Stadium, 2001

STU CLIBURN (Former Major League Pitcher; Minor League Coach) "In 1979, I was pitching for the Portland Beavers, the Triple-A team for the Pittsburgh Pirates. Stan, my twin brother, was a catcher for the Salt Lake City Gulls, the California Angels' Triple-A team. So Stan comes into Portland, and I happened to be starting that night. Stan was the catcher for the Gulls. Stan came to bat, and I got to face him for the first time in our professional careers. There was a big buildup in the papers: 'Twins Face Each Other for First Time.' His first at bat he swings at the first pitch, and it's over in like two seconds. He popped up to first base. We did face each other ten more times, and he'll be the first to tell you he got three hits. So he's a .300 hitter against his twin brother, Stu."

JOEL BENNETT (Former Major League Pitcher)

"We're coming from Columbus, traveling to Toledo. Triple-A, we take two buses. We checked out of the hotel, we bring all of our luggage in vans; we didn't have the buses yet. So all of our luggage was stored at the stadium. We get done with the game, we load up two buses. About halfway through the trip, somehow the buses get separated. On our bus, they're having a little bit of fun in the back, a few too many beers. It's pouring rain. One of the guys decides to light up a cigar. Brilliant idea. We all start screaming at him, 'cause the bus is filled with smoke. So he tries to lift the back hatch at the top of the bus to let the smoke out. As he undoes the handles, *Pffftttt!*—the wind yanked it right out of his hand. The whole hatch flew off, probably bouncing down the highway. Meantime, it's pouring rain, gallons of water pouring in. He runs up to the front to get some garbage bags, trying to cover all the seats. We get to Toledo a half-hour later than the first bus. They're all standing around waiting for us—the luggage was on our bus. We open the hatches—there's nothing in there. We left our luggage in Columbus. By this time, it's one thirty, two in the morning,

half of them are drunk, screaming and hollering. The bus driver is screaming at us. The next morning, the clubhouse guy who forgot to load our luggage had to run a van and drive all our luggage out. It was only an hour and a half, but I'll never forget that trip."

Cooper Stadium

COOPER STADIUM

◆ Home of the Columbus Clippers
(International League, Triple-A)

◆ Location—1155 West Mound Street, Columbus, Ohio

◆ Opened (as Red Bird Stadium)—1932

◆ Cost—$450,000

◆ Renovated (then named Franklin County Stadium)—1977

◆ Seating Capacity—15,000

◆ LF 355 CF 400 RF 330

Among the ballplayers who played here are Bernie Williams, Derek Jeter, Andy Pettitte, and Alfonso Soriano.

Ira Rosen

ALFONSO SORIANO (Major League Player) "I liked Columbus, the city. Trey Hillman was my manager [in Triple-A]; he was a real good guy. It was very tough. I played in Japan first. The language was difficult, talking about baseball."

DANNY SHEAFFER (Former Major League Player) "Back in 1998, we were in Columbus playing the Clippers. I was with the Pawtucket Red Sox. They have an AstroTurf field in Columbus, and we had an hour and a half rain delay, where several of the players tapped into the keg early, before the game was called. I wasn't one of them, but due to the fact we were not going to be able to compete in that game if it continued, I mysteriously placed the distributor wires from the Zamboni where they could not be found. When they couldn't start the machine, the game was postponed due to 'weather.' "

DOUG JENNINGS (Former Major League Player) "When I was in Rochester, they called up one of the kids. He had never been to the big leagues before, he was so excited. They brought him down to Baltimore. He was waiting in the hotel. But the guy they were supposed to put on the DL [to make room for the kid] refused to go. So the kid ended up not getting put on the major league roster. He came back to the minor leagues, his demeanor, his whole attitude changed. He became so frustrated, he was out of the game in two years."

AARON GETTYS (LouSeal [Lucille], the Columbus Clippers' Mascot) "I've been here three years. This is the first year that I took over full-time with the seal. It's a lot of fun. It puts you in a really good mood, seeing everybody's face. You get to make a fool out of yourself on the dugout and dance, and nobody knows who you are. I never thought about [this] as a career move, but if the opportunity was there for the major leagues, I'd probably take it."

CHRIS TRUBY (Major League Player) "The best part is the people you meet. You meet a lot people, make a lot of friends. The worst thing is the travel. Bus rides, early morning plane rides. The little things you might take for granted while you're up there, you realize it's not that easy down here."

Chris Truby, Durham Bulls, Cooper Stadium, 2003

Dunn Tire Park

DUNN TIRE PARK

- *Home of the Buffalo Bisons (International League, Triple-A)*

- *Location—275 Washington Street, Buffalo, New York*

- *Opening Day—April 14, 1988*

- *Cost—$56 million*

- *Seating Capacity—18,150*

- *LF 325 CF 404 RF 325*

Dunn Tire Park was originally named Pilot Field, then briefly called North AmeriCare Park. Among the ballplayers who played here are Richie Sexson, Bartolo Colon, and Brian Giles.

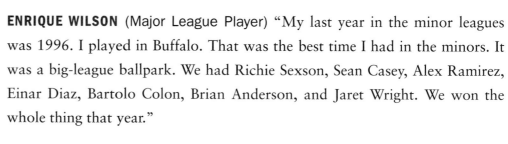

ENRIQUE WILSON (Major League Player) "My last year in the minor leagues was 1996. I played in Buffalo. That was the best time I had in the minors. It was a big-league ballpark. We had Richie Sexson, Sean Casey, Alex Ramirez, Einar Diaz, Bartolo Colon, Brian Anderson, and Jaret Wright. We won the whole thing that year."

NED YOST (Former Major League Player; Major League Manager) "Even in Triple-A, where you get to fly everywhere, you have to get up at 4:00 a.m.— and most flights fly the day of the game—or at 5:00 a.m. to catch the flight to

Ira Rosen

the next city. In the big leagues you fly right after the game, you're there at night. Uniforms are handed down from the major leagues. Your balls are old balls from the majors. When I managed in the minors, it was a great day when we got a box of old BP balls. Half our pitchers would be on the field during BP, shagging balls, the other half would be over the fence shagging home runs to save balls."

Phil Nevin, San Diego Padres, Petco Park, 2004

JOHN FLAHERTY (Former Major League Player) "I didn't think I had a chance to play in the big leagues, and if I was going to play pro ball, I wanted my family to be able to see as much of it as they could. I signed for $5,000. I knew I had a lot of things to work on. For me, it was more go and play and have fun and see what happens. I had a great year in Winter Haven, Florida—the Florida State League—I started thinking, maybe I had a chance. Then they threw me up to Triple-A. I got totally over-matched and thought I didn't have a chance. There were a lot of peaks and valleys. I didn't know I truly belonged until I got a chance in Detroit in 1995 to play every day and did well. That's when I stopped looking over my shoulder as the guy who was going back down. It took a lot of years, a lot of big league years before you finally believe it."

PHIL NEVIN (Major League Player) "I came out of college, I was drafted [by the Astros] as a power guy. I just didn't have the strength and the physical abilities to do the things that guys like [Jeff] Bagwell were doing. I was trying to hit home runs from the get-go, going up trying to hit a six-run homer. I got away from the things I was able to do, ability-wise. It was a learning process. It takes some people longer to figure it out than others."

Frontier Field

FRONTIER FIELD

- ◆ Home of the Rochester Red Wings
  (International League, Triple-A)

- ◆ Location—One Morrie Silver Way, Rochester, New York

- ◆ Opening Day—June 27, 1997

- ◆ Cost—$35.3 million

- ◆ Seating Capacity—10,840

- ◆ LF 335 CF 402 RF 325

In 1997 Frontier Field replaced Silver Stadium, which was known as Red
Wing Stadium from 1929 to 1967. Among the ballplayers who played here
are B. J. Ryan, Jose Mesa, and Brian Roberts.

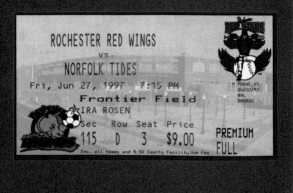

ROCHESTER RED WINGS
vs.
NORFOLK TIDES
Fri, Jun 27, 1997 7:15 PM
Frontier Field
IRA ROSEN
Sec Row Seat Price
115   D   3 $9.00   PREMIUM
                          FULL
Inc. all taxes and $.50 County Facility Use Fee

GARY COHEN (Broadcaster) "Life in the minor leagues is interesting. When I was doing games in Spartanburg and Durham in A-ball, you're *so far* from the major leagues that you can't even see it. There's an incredible sense of camaraderie among the players at that level. But it's very different at Triple-A, because you're so close to the major leagues, a lot of the guys who are there have either been there already, aspire to get there, or are on their way down. No one's ever satisfied being in Triple-A. Which makes Triple-A the hardest

Ira Rosen

managerial job that there is. If you can manage in Triple-A and be successful, you can manage anywhere."

KHALIL GREENE (Major League Player) "The camaraderie in the locker room—for me that was one of the funnest things. Everybody is the same age demographic so there's a lot in common. When you get to the [major league] level it's a little bit more spread out. Everyone's got their certain interests—wives and families and whatnot. The guys I came up with, I talk to them all the time; Jake Gautreau, Michael Johnson, Henri Stanley. It was a good time. You have to motivate yourself because the crowd isn't there. The sense of urgency is less—the room for error [in the majors] is very small. You're accountable for everything you do. You're not in that development stage; you're expected to perform."

MARK SMITH (Former Major League Player) "I [still] think I can help out a big-league team. I got off to a bad start [this year], but I'm hitting the ball good now, and I think I could be a viable right-handed hitter off the bench. I've got a wife I married in 2000 and a baby on the way. [After baseball] it's nine to five. I'm not going to have the money to retire and play golf the rest of my life. Going to finish my degree—I've got five classes left."

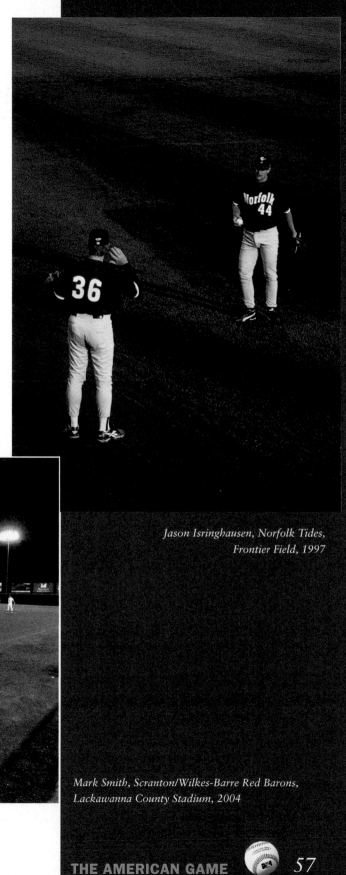

Jason Isringhausen, Norfolk Tides,
Frontier Field, 1997

Mark Smith, Scranton/Wilkes-Barre Red Barons,
Lackawanna County Stadium, 2004

Knights Stadium

KNIGHTS STADIUM

- *Home of the Charlotte Knights
  (International League, Triple-A)*

- *Location—Gold Hill Road at I-77, Fort Mill, South Carolina*

- *Opened—1990*

- *Cost—$15 million*

- *Seating Capacity—10,002*

- *LF 326 CF 400 RF 325*

Also known as Knights Castle. Among the ballplayers who played here are Manny Ramirez, Jim Thome, and Livan Hernandez.

TODD WALKER (Major League Player) "The minor leagues are what baseball is all about. You're not making a lot of money, you're just playing with a dream. When you get to the big leagues, you still continue to work hard, but it's not the same as the minor leagues. You put a lot of time in . . . I think that's what fans appreciate. You definitely earn it when you get to the big leagues."

Ira Rosen

CRAIG BRAZELL (Minor League Player) "I grew up around the game. My father was with the Detroit Tigers in the minor leagues for fourteen years as a player and manager. I had a good idea coming into this game what it was about. I was directly out of high school into professional baseball. The biggest transition for me was being away from home for so long. You're gone six or seven months at a time. I didn't have my father there to talk to after every game in person, to critique what I did that night. The ultimate goal for myself is to have fun and to play in the big leagues. To be on ESPN. If you don't have fun playing the game, you'll bury yourself."

CHAD MOTTOLA (Former Major League Player) "It was eleven years ago. I was taken in the first round. Came into baseball, still enjoying the game so I'm still playing. I still play the game because I feel I can still have success in it. I wouldn't be playing just to pass the time. Unfortunately, at my age I need things to happen for me to go up. I just can't control my own destiny now. I'm thirty-one. I'd love to settle down—I've been dating a girl now for a while—but I don't feel like dragging her into this mess that I'm in right now."

Craig Brazell, Norfolk Tides, Lackawanna County Stadium, 2004

Lackawanna County Stadium

LACKAWANNA COUNTY STADIUM

- *Home of the Scranton/Wilkes-Barre Red Barons (International League, Triple-A)*

- *Location—235 Montage Mountain Road, Moosic, Pennsylvania*

- *Opening Day—April 26, 1989*

- *Cost—$25 million*

- *Seating Capacity—10,982*

- *LF 330 CF 408 RF 330*

Among the ballplayers who played here are Chase Utley, Pat Burrell, and Ryan Madson.

RYAN MADSON (Major League Pitcher) "You've got to take in what people say to you, what they're trying to help you with. It's kind of a long haul. You're trying to make a life, a career out of baseball."

JOSE VALENTIN (Major League Player) "For Spanish people, it's the language. You have to learn English. You have to be able to buy groceries, to know where you're at walking around. I came here when I was seventeen years old, I

Ira Rosen

wasn't able to speak English. It was real hard, but I forced myself to do it. That's the only way I can communicate with my teammates. I signed with the Padres. My first three years, they had a Spanish teacher in the spring training complex. You'd go two days a week. It helped."

Jose Valentin, Chicago White Sox,
Fenway Park, 2004

Ryan Madson, Reading Phillies,
FirstEnergy Stadium, 2002

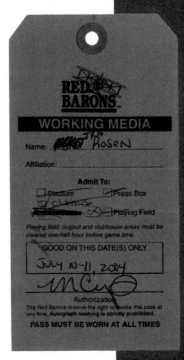

McCoy Stadium

McCOY STADIUM

- Home of the Pawtucket Red Sox
  (International League, Triple-A)

- Location—Ben Mondor Way, Pawtucket, Rhode Island

- Opened—1942

- Renovated—1998–1999

- Seating Capacity—10,031

- LF 325 CF 400 RF 325

McCoy Stadium was the site of the longest game in professional baseball history—32 innings on April 18, 1981. Cal Ripken played in that game. Among the ballplayers who played here are Nomar Garciaparra, Wade Boggs, and Roger Clemens.

TODD WILLIAMS (Major League Pitcher) "I got drafted in 1991 by the Dodgers. I remember going into A-ball, calling my parents and saying, 'I'll be in A-ball this year, maybe next year. Hopefully, in Double-A in a couple of years.' Two months later, I'm in Double-A. After my first full year, I'm in the Fall League with Piazza, the big guys then. Next year I'm in Triple-A, and it was like a screeching halt. They keep telling you every single day, 'Hey, we want you [up] there.' Instead of paying other guys a million dollars to do the same thing. But they tell you that for three years. They keep coming up with

Ira Rosen

excuses—you're not throwing another pitch, work on this, work on that . . . It *was* fun, it *was* a game. Then you're at Triple-A, you learn so much more about the business. Then you can't treat it as a game anymore."

TYLER YATES (Major League Pitcher) "When you get to the big leagues, it's like a dream come true. Getting sent back down, I know I have a lot of work ahead of me. What was difficult for me was starting—I had to learn how to be a starting pitcher in the big leagues. That's the reason I'm not there any-more. My arm couldn't handle all the innings. [Now] I'm a reliever again. When they feel I'm ready, that's their call. The biggest difference is the pres-sure to win. In the minors, a lot of systems encourage winning but also devel-opment. The pressure to win is not as great."

SEAN CASEY (Major League Player) "It's funny—at the time, I didn't enjoy the bus rides. Looking back, probably my *best* memory was the bus rides—doubling up, people sleeping on the floor. When I was in Double-A, we had a sixteen-hour bus ride from Portland, Maine, to Akron, Ohio. I enjoyed the camaraderie with the guys. My first year in pro ball, we won the championship in Watertown, New York. That was pretty cool. We made like $800 a month. Then in 1997 in Buffalo, my last game in the minors, I hit the game-winning home run in the tenth inning to win the champi-onship in Triple-A. I got called to the big leagues the next day, been here ever since."

Tyler Yates, Norfolk Tides,
Lackawanna County Stadium, 2004

Sean Casey, Cincinnati Reds, Great
American Ballpark, 2003

PART THREE

DOUBLE-A

Double-A is the second highest level of Minor League Baseball. As in Triple-A, there are thirty teams, one for each franchise in Major League Baseball. Double-A consists of three leagues: the Eastern League, with twelve teams; the Southern League, with ten teams; and the Texas League, with eight teams. Reaching the Double-A level is a numbers game, since there are twice as many teams in Single-A, Full Season. Many of the best prospects in baseball can be found here, and they often make the jump directly to the big leagues, bypassing Triple-A, and the possible negative influence of certain veteran players who don't want to be there.

FirstEnergy Stadium

FIRSTENERGY STADIUM

- *Home of the Reading Phillies (Eastern League, Double-A)*

- *Location—Centre Avenue and Route 61 South, Reading, Pennsylvania*

- *Opening Day—May 28, 1951*

- *Seating Capacity—9,100*

- *LF 330   CF 400   RF 330*

Originally named Reading Municipal Memorial Stadium, the park was renamed GPU Stadium in 1999 and named FirstEnergy Stadium before the 2002 season. Among the ballplayers who played here are Mike Schmidt, Ryne Sandberg, and Scott Rolen.

DAVE LaPOINT (Former Major League Pitcher; Minor League Coach) "In 2000 we were on a bus trip going into Shreveport, Louisiana, from Texas. It's the middle of the night, and of course the air conditioning doesn't work, which it never does on any of the buses in the Texas League. We get about one hundred miles outside of town and the back of the bus catches on fire. The exhaust is coming into the bus, so there's twenty-six guys sitting up front 'cause they don't want to breathe the fumes. One of the pistons blew, so the gas leaking out the back catches on fire. So we pull into Shreveport, and the

Ira Rosen

cops spot us and it's like a SWAT team: 'Get out of the bus, you're on fire!' 'We know we're on fire, we've been traveling for an hour on fire, we're just trying to make it to our hotel room, please let us go, it's only two miles.' And they did!"

SCARBOROUGH GREEN (Former Major League Player) "Texas League, 1998. Driving from Jackson, Mississippi, to Shreveport, Louisiana. The heat index was around 120 degrees. Two hours into the trip, the air-conditioning goes off. The driver pulls off the road, tries to fix it, but the bus breaks down. Out in the middle of nowhere for four hours. We ended up getting to the game about a half-hour before it started, and *we won*."

DAVE TOMLIN (Former Major League Pitcher; Minor League Coach) "I was in the Southern League, playing Double-A baseball with the Cincinnati Reds. We had to go from Asheville, North Carolina, to Mobile, Alabama, after a game. We left about 11:00, 11:30 p.m., drive down toward Atlanta. After about three and a half, four hours, bus driver says, 'I gotta get some coffee so I can stay awake.' Most of the players on the bus are sleeping. I'm sitting in the second row. I look up and see a sign—Atlanta 35 miles. Bus driver comes back, players go back to sleep. I wake up about two hours later. I look up, sign says, Atlanta 115 miles. Driver went the wrong way, back toward Asheville."

Scarborough Green, New Haven Ravens, Yale Field, 2001

 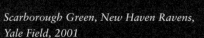

The sign reads: ITs My 7th Birthday. Can I Be In The Starting Line Up? Please

PAUL HEMPHILL (Author) "The war was over, but the steel mills still boomed in Birmingham, Alabama, where the Barons of the Class AA Southern League were the favored entertainment for the city's boisterous blue-collar masses. They played at old Rickwood Field on the cindery fringe of the 'Pittsburgh of the South,' and late in the 1947 season, at the age of eleven I went there with my father for a Sunday doubleheader against the Mobile Bears."

"That first glimpse of Rickwood's emerald grass and silvery light standards was dazzling, but I most remember the crowd. Survivors of the war and the mills, they felt they deserved better than this bunch. They had heckled as the woeful Barons lost the first game, but they turned belligerent by the fifth inning of the second when the homeboys were being bombed again. A shower of rental cushions began to cover the field, and soon the umpire ruled a forfeit and everybody went home mad. I knew then that baseball was a lot more than a game."

JACKIE HERNANDEZ (Former Major League Player; Minor League Coach) "I played in the minor leagues five years, from 1961 to 1965. I think my hardest year was 1963 in the Eastern League, when I played in Charleston. We had to travel twelve, fourteen, eighteen hours when we left Charleston to come to Springfield, Massachusetts, and Binghamton, New York. But I enjoyed it very much because we won the championship."

Jackie Hernandez, New Jersey Jackals,
Yogi Berra Stadium, 2002

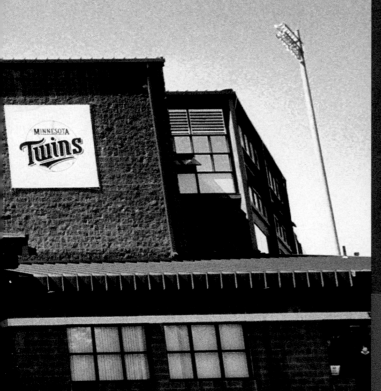

New Britain Stadium

NEW BRITAIN STADIUM

- *Home of the New Britain Rock Cats*
  (Eastern League, Double-A)

- *Location—230 John Karbonic Way, New Britain, Connecticut*

- *Opening Day—April 12, 1996*

- *Seating Capacity—6,146*

- *LF 330 CF 400 RF 330*

New Britain Stadium replaced Beehive Field, which was built in 1982.
Among the ballplayers who played here are Torii Hunter, Jacque Jones,
Michael Cuddyer, and Juan Rincon.

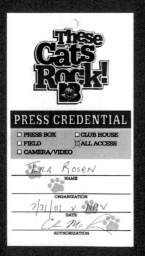

Ira Rosen

ROBIN ROBERTS (Hall of Fame Pitcher) "My first trip to the minors after signing with the Phillies, I was at Wilmington, Delaware. The Wilmington Blue Rocks in the Interstate League. I was on an excellent club, I was 9-1. They called me up to the big leagues on June 17. My second experience was at the end of my career. I was trying to hook on with somebody after I'd been released. I decided I would go down to Reading in the Phillies farm system and pitch there till June 15; if nobody picked me up, I'd go home. Well, they didn't pick me up and I went home. I was 5-3, pitched decent. But I was forty years old. . . . I've got to say, I respect so much the amount of effort that goes into the minor leagues."

MICHAEL CUDDYER (Major League Player) "After I was first drafted, the Twins sent me up to Minnesota for BP, infield, to see what it was like in Minneapolis. First day in the locker room, Paul Molitor and Pat Meares were there. I was drafted as a shortstop, so Molitor turns to Meares and says, 'So, Mearsie, this is the guy that's going to take your spot, huh?' I'm sitting there, eighteen years old, my mouth is shut. And Meares says, 'In five years he can have it.' The funny thing is, when Molitor was eighteen years old, same situation. He came to Milwaukee with the Brewers, Sal Bando said the same thing to Robin Yount: 'Here's the guy that's going to take your job.' The next year, Molitor did take it—they moved Yount. And Molitor's been waiting twenty years to use that line! It made me feel special, bring in an eighteen-year-old kid out of high school, to go up to Minnesota and have a future Hall of Famer say something like that."

JOE FERGUSON (Former Major League Player; Minor League Manager) "Probably the most rewarding part for any manager in the minor leagues is to see a player go to the big leagues that you had something to do with his development. I've only been in the minor leagues for seven years, so I probably don't have as many players that have gone to the big leagues as other minor league people. Probably the first that has made an impact would be David Dellucci with the Arizona Diamondbacks. I had him in Double-A; he was struggling the first month of the season. We made some changes with him; he was an excellent athlete, great work ethic. He went from hitting .120 in May to about .350 in June and then went to the big leagues with Baltimore. For me, that was a great

Michael Cuddyer, New Britain RockCats,
New Britain Stadium, 2001

Juan Rincon, New Britain RockCats,
New Britain Stadium, 2001

experience, very rewarding to see a young player like that get something so quickly, have success."

JUAN RINCON (Major League Pitcher) "Back in 1999, I never had enough money to bring my family here [from Venezuela]. You spend six, seven months without seeing them, not even have money to call them. That's very sad, because sometimes you need somebody to talk with, somebody who loves you. Besides that, you make trips for twelve hours on a bus. It's no fun at all. Some of the ballparks are very old. A lot of people back home think that I'm having the best life, riding a limo or going to the ballpark in a helicopter. Having a lot of money. It's 180 degrees opposite that. So when you realize that you have some tools here and you have a taste of major league life, you just need to keep working. But there's a lot of pain you've got to go through to get there, knowing you may not get there. I played with forty guys my first year, only two of us are left."

ED HEARN (Former Major League Player) "I spent eight and a half years getting to the major leagues. After I hurt my shoulder, [the Royals] sent me back on rehab to Omaha. Then I was released and signed with the Indians. They sent me to Double-A. Means long bus rides, Eastern League. They said I'd be there two weeks. Turned into the All-Star break. I said, 'I'm not taking another one of them stinking bus rides.' We went from London, Ontario, to Canton, Ohio. Ten hours. I said, 'I'm outta here.'"

RICO BROGNA (Former Major League Player; Minor League Coach) "When you're a player, your goal is to get better to make the big leagues. As a hitting coach in Double-A, my aspirations are not quite the same. Here it's more of a selfless attitude I think I have. [I] help players to help them realize their dreams. You find out a lot about people, about work ethic, dedication. I'm not sure where the road I'm taking is going . . . see what happens."

Rico Brogna, Reading Phillies,
FirstEnergy Stadium, 2002

NYSEG Stadium

NYSEG STADIUM

- *Home of the Binghamton Mets
  (Eastern League, Double-A)*

- *Location—211 Henry Street, Binghamton, New York*

- *Opened—1992*

- *Seating Capacity—6,012*

- *LF 330 CF 400 RF 330*

NYSEG Stadium was originally named Binghamton Municipal Stadium. Among the ballplayers who played here are Jose Reyes, Edgardo Alfonzo, and Jason Isringhausen.

GAME 50

FIRST BASE

10	J	4
SEC	ROW	SEAT

NYSEG
STADIUM
Mets
VS.
NEW HAVEN
RAVENS

THURSDAY
JULY 25, 2002
7:00 PM

GAME TIME SUBJECT TO CHANGE
NO REFUND • NO EXCHANGE
RAIN CHECK POLICY
IN THE EVENT 4-1/2 INNINGS ARE NOT PLAYED
ON THIS DATE, MAY BE EXCHANGED FOR ANY
NON-RESTRICTED 2002 REGULAR SEASON GAME,
BASED ON AVAILABILITY.

GAME 50

FIRST BASE

10	J	4
SEC	ROW	SEAT

ROLLIE FINGERS (Hall of Fame Pitcher) "Birmingham, Alabama, opening day, 1967. Guy hit a line drive back at me. Hit me in the face. I was out two and a half months. I faced him two and half months later—hit him right in the ribs. He wasn't going to hit me again."

JOSE REYES (Major League Player) "[How does it feel to be a top Mets prospect?] I really don't give it that much thought. I just have to go out there and play my game. This is my third year [2002]. I expect to get to the big leagues in one year."

Jose Reyes, Binghamton Mets,
NYSEG Stadium, 2002

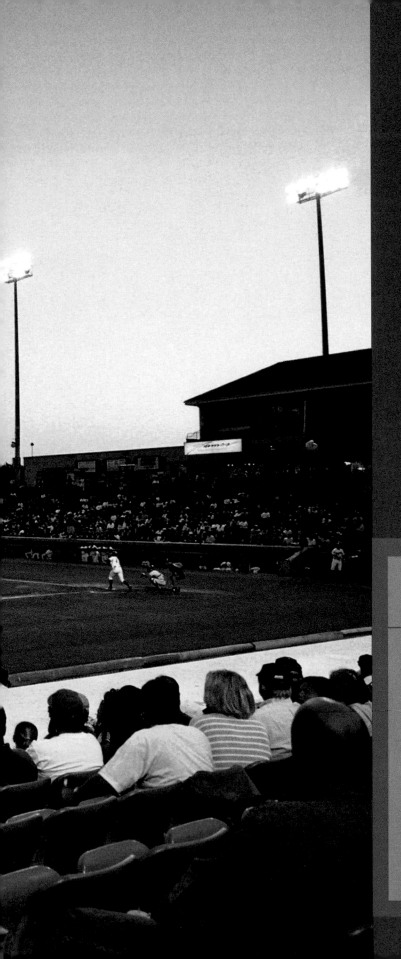

Thomas Dodd Stadium

SENATOR THOMAS J. DODD MEMORIAL STADIUM

- *Home of the Connecticut Defenders (formerly the Norwich Navigators) (Eastern League, Double-A)*

- *Location—14 Stott Avenue, Norwich, Connecticut*

- *Opening Day—April 17, 1995*

- *Cost—$9.3 Million*

- *Seating Capacity—6,270*

- *LF 309 CF 401 RF 309*

Among the ballplayers who played here are Mike Lowell, Eric Milton, and Alfonso Soriano.

2001

MEDIA PASS

GOOD FOR ADMITTANCE TO:
**PRESS BOX, FIELD,
CLUBHOUSE & ROVING**

NOT GOOD FOR SEAT

Ira Rosen
NAME

AFFILIATION

July 30
GOOD THIS DATE ONLY

THIS PASS IS ISSUED SUBJECT TO CONDITIONS
SET FORTH ON THE BACK HEREOF

NOT TRANSFERRABLE

90   Ira Rosen

POKEY REESE (Major League Player) "My favorite place to play was Chattanooga, Tennessee—the Lookouts—Double-A ball. I played two years there. I enjoyed the time with my teammates, those ten- and twelve-hour bus rides. It was probably the best times in baseball for me, other than now."

BRAD WILKERSON (Major League Player) "I struggled my first year in Double-A. Our team was six or seven games back in the Eastern League. [Then] I started swinging the bat better. Everyone started playing better. We ended up going to the playoffs. The Milton Bradley grand slam, 3-2, two outs against Norwich in the ninth inning that won it in the rain at Harrisburg—it was the most exciting time I've had in baseball."

KEVIN MILLAR (Major League Player) "In Minor League Baseball, you always have the fun stuff between innings. You had dogs bringing out the balls, massages on the dugouts. My favorite home fields were Kane County in Chicago and the Portland Sea Dogs. It brings the coziness to baseball—the fans can relate to minor leaguers."

*Brad Wilkerson, Montreal Expos,
Citizens Bank Park, 2004*

Waterfront Park

WATERFRONT PARK

- *Home of the Trenton Thunder*
  (Eastern League, Double-A)

- *Location—One Thunder Road, Trenton, New Jersey*

- *Opening Day—May 9, 1994*

- *Cost—$20 million*

- *Seating Capacity—6,440*

- *LF 330 CF 407 RF 330*

The official name of this stadium is Samuel J. Plumeri, Sr. Field at Mercer County Waterfront Park. Among the ballplayers who played here are Nomar Garciaparra, Shea Hillenbrand, and Tony Clark.

Ira Rosen

JAYSON STARK (Writer, Broadcaster) "I went to a game in Trenton a few years back. Somebody hit a ball in the shortstop hole. And a guy I'd barely heard of named Nomar Garciaparra went in the hole—this was a play that most shortstops would have eaten—and Nomar was there and totally under control. And then that ball came flying out of his hand. I think it was faster than the speed of sound. I never forgot that play. All you had to do was to see the way he made that play to know that this was a guy who was going places."

NOMAR GARCIAPARRA (Major League Player) "I remember my first manager and coach in A-Ball, DeMarlo Hale and Al Nipper. I remember Pawtucket, how great the owners were, the fans were unbelievable."

LYLE OVERBAY (Major League Player) "I liked the Round Rock stadium in Double-A. The fans are great—it didn't matter who you played for, they just wanted to watch a good game. If you made a good play against them, they wouldn't boo you. It was fun to play against them."

JAKE PEAVY (Major League Pitcher) "I played in my hometown, Mobile. What a wonderful experience, to have my friends and family watch me play. Not many players get to do that. You wanted to do good—on any given night, there would be five hundred people there that knew you personally."

Jake Peavy, Petco Park, 2004

PART FOUR

SINGLE-A, FULL SEASON

There are two levels in this classification: High-A and Low-A. High-A has thirty teams, one for each franchise in Major League Baseball. It consists of three leagues: the California League, with ten teams; the Carolina League, with eight teams; and the Florida State League, with twelve teams. The competition at this level features more experienced players than at Low-A, which also has thirty teams, spread over two leagues: the Midwest League, with fourteen teams; and the South Atlantic League, with sixteen teams. Only about 5 percent of the ballplayers who reach this level will ever play in the big leagues.

Arrowhead Credit Union Park

ARROWHEAD CREDIT UNION PARK

◆ *Home of the Inland Empire 66ers*
  (California League, Single-A)

◆ *Location—280 South E Street, San Bernardino, California*

◆ *Opening Day—August 26, 1996*

◆ *Cost—$16.5 million*

◆ *Seating Capacity—5,000*

◆ *LF 330 CF 410 RF 330*

Also known as the Ranch, this ballpark was originally named San Bernardino Stadium. Among the ballplayers who played here are Adrian Beltre and Ted Lilly.

STAN CLIBURN (Former Major League Player; Minor League Manager) "I was managing in the Carolina League in 1991. In Peninsula, where the Class A club of the Seattle Mariners was: very dreary ballpark. Fred Stanley at the time was a roving minor league instructor with Seattle. He was a friend of mine back in the major league days when I was with the Angels and he was with Seattle. We went out late one night and turned the sprinkler heads on, left the water on all night. So we got the day off the next day in Peninsula!"

JOSH BECKETT (Major League Pitcher) "The most fun is the camaraderie with the guys. The funniest thing that's happened: this last year [2000], a belt came off, started smelling up the bus. All of the Latin guys sat in the back last year at Kane County. I remember Stevie Morales running toward the front of the bus, making sheep noises—'Baaaaa, baaaaa.' You sit back and look at it like, 'This is so much more fun than having a real job.'"

RAMON AVILES (Former Major League Player; Minor League Coach) "Coaching in the minor leagues, the thing that is significant for us [is] when we help a kid and see him grow through the year—how he started in spring training, how much progress he made . . . we are very proud of him, he's like our son. I remember when Jimmy Rollins, shortstop for the Philadelphia Phillies, signed with us out of high school, eighteen years old. He started in Martinsville, Virginia, when I was the infield instructor for the organization at that time. Seeing him grow every year, mature, it was great. All-Star Game, two years in a row. I'm very proud of him, because he worked hard, day in and day out all his career in the minor leagues, and he still does so in the major leagues."

Josh Beckett, Portland Sea Dogs,
Thomas Dodd Stadium, 2001

Fifth Third Field

FIFTH THIRD FIELD

- ◆ *Home of the Dayton Dragons (Midwest League, Single-A)*
- ◆ *Location—First Street, Dayton, Ohio*
- ◆ *Opening Day—April 27, 2000*
- ◆ *Cost—$23.1 million*
- ◆ *Seating Capacity—7,230*
- ◆ *LF 338 CF 402 RF 338*

Among the ballplayers who played here are Adam Dunn and Austin Kearns.

  Ira Rosen

ADAM DUNN (Major League Player) "If people haven't been to Dayton, it's one of the best stadiums in the minor leagues by far."

PAUL BLAIR (Former Major League Player) "I played three years in the minor leagues—Stockton, Elmira, and Santa Barbara. The thing I remember most is my first year in Santa Barbara. It was the first time I ever played night baseball. For a seventeen-year old kid to play professional baseball was something you never forget."

KEVIN HOWARD (Minor League Player) "When I came to professional baseball, I was expecting it to be a little worse [than college]. You hear war stories about how minor league ball is tough, the bus rides. It really hasn't been that bad. Dayton is one of the best places to play. It's not that much different from Miami, where I played in college."

JOSH WHETZEL (Broadcaster) "The first team that I worked for, in Albany, Georgia, had Vladimir Guerrero, Brad Fullmer, Javier Vasquez, and about ten guys overall that have played in the major leagues. With all those players on an A-Ball team that wound up playing in the majors, the ball club still finished about fifteen games under .500. Which goes to prove, in the minor leagues you can have all the talent in the world and it doesn't always translate into a winning team, because a lot of times you manage differently. It's more about development than it is winning."

RALPH KINER (Hall of Fame Player; Broadcaster) "I came to the minors in 1941. I started out at Albany in the Eastern League, Class-A, third highest in baseball, out of high school. I made *$150 a month*. That's what I remember most."

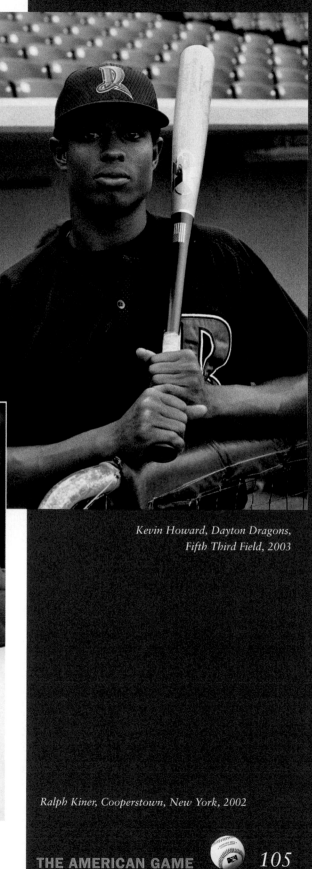

Kevin Howard, Dayton Dragons,
Fifth Third Field, 2003

Ralph Kiner, Cooperstown, New York, 2002

FirstEnergy Park

FIRSTENERGY PARK

- *Home of the Lakewood BlueClaws (South Atlantic League, Single-A)*

- *Location—New Hampshire Avenue and Stadium Way, Lakewood, New Jersey*

- *Opening Day—April 11, 2001*

- *Cost—$22 million*

- *Seating Capacity—6,588*

- *LF 325 CF 400 RF 325*

Originally named GPU Energy Park. Among the ballplayers who played here are Ryan Howard and Gavin Floyd.

MEDIA

LAKEWOOD
BlueClaws
™

DAILY PASS

Name **Ira Rosen**
Affiliation **Author**
Date **July 15th, 2002**

Ira Rosen

BRIAN McRAE (Former Major League Player) "I still keep in touch with a lot of guys that I played Rookie Ball and A-ball with. It was a fun time. You're seventeen, eighteen years old, you don't know any better. You're in remote places in the United States. I played in Eugene, Oregon, my first year. It was fun, riding the buses, making five dollars a day meal money. Everybody thinks you graduate [high school] and get to the big leagues, and you're making a lot of money. They don't realize how much guys sacrifice in the minor leagues, and how much hard work and time is put in riding the buses, staying in bad hotels—it's not as plush as people think it is."

TODD COFFEY (Major League Pitcher) "I got drafted in 1998 by the Reds. I went in the forty-first round out of high school. I was seventeen years old.

Signed on a Sunday, that Tuesday I was on a plane out to Montana. I pretty much grew up into an adult in baseball. I had a setback in 1999—I had Tommy John arm surgery, so I missed two years. [Making it to the big leagues] you get hints here and there, but if you go out and put up your numbers, that's all you've got to do."

CHRIS JAILE (Minor League Player) "I was drafted in 1999 out of Christopher Columbus High School in Miami, Florida, in the fourth round. Went directly to Rookie Ball, Gulf Coast League in Florida. Since then, I went to my first

spring training as a nineteen-year-old. Unfortunately, I got hurt. Spent about three months on the DL. This is my fourth season, last two seasons in High-A with the Port Charlotte Rangers in the Florida State League. This year I had pretty high hopes of going up to Double-A. Last year I had an unlucky year with the bat—hit below .200. In spring training this year, got brought up to the major league camp nine times. Got a base hit against the Giants. They made an organizational move two days before spring training was over, brought in another catcher and sent me to Low-A [Clinton LumberKings, Midwest League], so I could play every day. I've been a platoon guy, so they

Ira Rosen

said, 'Go out and catch a hundred-plus games. Come to spring training next year, fight for a big-league job.' This is not a demotion, this is a good opportunity."

CHARLEY STEINER (Broadcaster) "My second professional job, I was working in Davenport, Iowa, at radio station KSTT. The Quad Cities Angels were the ball club that I covered. The stadium was right on the banks of the Mississippi—the one that floods all the time. It's like war and pestilence converging, with rats and the water that's up into the dugouts. Like going down into a swimming pool. The best part was in 1971. They had a young, flame-throwing phenom that they were so high on in the Angel organization. Billy Moffett, who was the pitching coach for the Angels' major league club would fly to Davenport every fifth day to watch this kid pitch. And it wasn't easy to get to Davenport, because there is no 'there' there. The kid's name was Frank Tanana. Watching Tanana pitch in this minor league ballpark and watching him develop into a great pitcher in his day before he got hurt—that was a thrill."

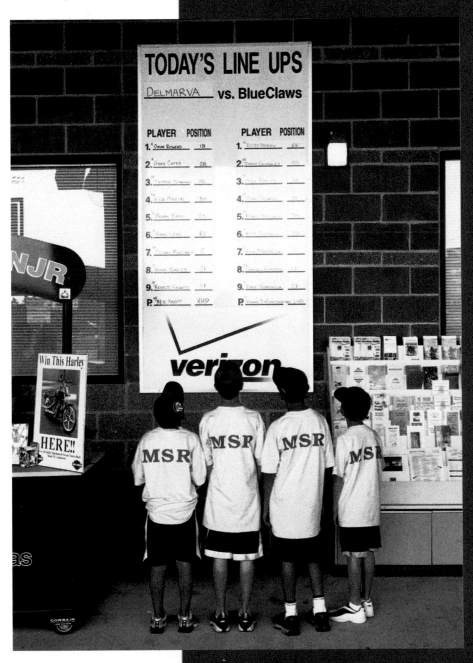

Harry Grove Stadium

HARRY GROVE STADIUM

- ◆ *Home of the Frederick Keys*
  (Carolina League, Single-A)

- ◆ *Location—6201 New Design Road, Frederick, Maryland*

- ◆ *Opened—1990*

- ◆ *Seating Capacity—5,400*

- ◆ *LF 325 CF 400 RF 325*

Among the ballplayers who played here are Brady Anderson, Armando Benitez, and Arthur Rhodes.

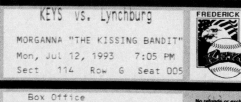

KEYS vs. Lynchburg

FREDERICK

MORGANNA "THE KISSING BANDIT"

Mon, Jul 12, 1993   7:05 PM
Sect   114   Row G   Seat 005

Box Office

No refunds or exchanges

114   Ira Rosen

BERNIE WILLIAMS (Major League Player) "[One of my favorite memories was] in Prince William, the Carolina League. I remember having a great time—I was still single. My mom was there, my dad was still alive; they spent a big part of the summer with me. We got a chance to meet some Latin American families that were there. We used to have barbecues all the time. It was a great time—no pressure, no fame. We didn't know about fast cars or 'red carpet' or big stadiums. We were just playing for the love of the game."

WILLIE RANDOLPH (Former Major League Player; Major League Manager) "The year that I thought I really kind of grew up as a man, I was in Thetford Mines, Canada. Small town in Quebec, middle of nowhere. Ten degrees outside. The field was a little bandbox. As a young player going away from home, you come to that defining moment, that place and time where you have to grow up as a man. I remember being real homesick and depressed about the weather and the culture—there was no English-speaking [people] in the town, it was all French-speaking [people]. I wanted to go home. My mom talked me out of it, telling me, 'You've got to step up, grow up.' I finally looked at myself in the mirror one day and said, 'Listen, if you're going to make it to the 'big show,' you're going to have to go through the tough times and deal with adversity and play the game.' That's when I thought I turned the corner. I actually made it to the big leagues kind of quick. I was in the big leagues at twenty-one. That was my Double-A year. The following year I spent a half-year in Triple-A, then the big leagues with the Pittsburgh Pirates in August 1975. I was able to adjust well, once I got there. The Yankees traded for me at the end of 1975—the rest is history."

RICH DONNELLY (Major League Coach) "First year I managed was 1972, Greenville Rangers in the [Texas] Rangers farm system. About a week before the season started they told me, 'Rich, we're sorry but the ballpark has just burned to the ground.' When I arrived in Greenville, all I found was a wall from foul line to foul line. A brick wall. That was it, there was no clubhouse, no stands. For that year, they put up a chicken net for the backstop about thirty feet behind home plate. I think we drew *eighty-four* people for the year. About two or three a game, maybe. I called it 'the Alamo' because people would put their ladders up on the right-field wall and come up over the wall to watch the game. Then about halfway into the season, we had a tremendous storm and the wall caved in from left-center to center field. So we put up a rope—onto the rope was a double, over the rope was a home run. It didn't make a difference—you couldn't see out there anyway, the lights were so bad. When Minor League Baseball sent around a guy with a light meter [to test the lights], he needed a flashlight to read the light meter."

PART FIVE

SINGLE-A, SHORT SEASON

Often called Rookie Ball, this classification consists of five leagues containing fifty-three teams. Players in the New York–Penn League, with fourteen teams, tend to have the most experience, having played in college or the Arizona League (nine teams) or the Gulf Coast League (twelve teams). There is also the Appalachian League, with ten teams, and the Northwest League, with eight teams. Schedules run between fifty-four and seventy-six games. Most ballplayers who sign professional contracts out of high school or who have limited college experience start at this level. Only approximately 1 percent of them will ever put on a major league uniform.

Dwyer Stadium

DWYER STADIUM

- *Home of the Batavia Muckdogs*
  (New York–Penn League, Single-A)

- *Location—299 Bank Street, Batavia, New York*

- *Opening Day—May 10, 1939*

- *Demolished—1995; replaced by new Dwyer Stadium built on the*
  same site, opened 1996

- *Seating Capacity—2,600*

- *LF 326 CF 382 RF 325*

Among the ballplayers who played here are Dock Ellis, Steve Blass, and
Andy Ashby.

GENERAL ADMISSION
1995
Championship
Season
NY-P League
Professional Baseball

Clippers

JUL 2 1995
Dwyer Stadium

Rain Check
In the event that 4 1/2 innings of
this game are not played, this ticket
may be exchanged at the box office
for an available ticket for any regular
season game.

No outside food or beverage allowed
in stadium.

Adult   Child

120   Ira Rosen

TIM FLANNERY (Former Major League Player; Major League Coach) "I managed four years in the minors before I started coaching third in the majors. I [once] got thrown out of a game in A-ball. I went back to my office, and the [team] mascot came through. I told him he was done, and hopped in the mascot suit. Went back and finished managing the team, and did a routine to 'Louie Louie.' Can't do that stuff at the major league level."

JOE McEWING (Major League Player) "The relationships that come from being with those guys every single day, more than your family. It's such a wonderful experience. The guys who I hung out with in A-ball I still talk to today—Brian Rupe, Pop Warner, John Mabry, Adam Kennedy. 'Foxhole people.'"

JOHN GALL (Major League Player) "The good and bad in Minor League Baseball is travel. My first season, we were in Ohio. We had a night game; the next day, we had a day game in Staten Island [New York]. We made that drive, got off the bus around 10:30 a.m. in Staten Island. Got the living day-lights beat out of us."

DANIEL TOSCA (Minor League Player) "You come here and everyone is about the same [talent]. Someone's trying to get your position every year. Playing minor league ball is tough. You don't get as much sleep as you'd like . . . you have to come to the ballpark ready to play, day-to-day. My uncle [Carlos Tosca] put his time in for twenty years or more. I kinda learned from that. He tells me that you've got to work harder than the hardest worker, and I think that's the key to it. It's not like I have a lot of tools—I have to work hard."

BROOKS BADEAUX (Minor League Player) "It's been a lot of fun. The most fun about it is you're chasing a dream to play in the big leagues, which is something not many people get to do. I'm a baseball fan myself or I wouldn't be playing. It helps with life. You have to handle the failures. When people finish playing, it puts you on a good path to be successful in anything you want to do in life. I have faith in myself, but things have to go your way. I'm not going to stop trying."

Daniel Tosca, Lakewood BlueClaws, FirstEnergy Park, 2002

Damaschke Field

DAMASCHKE FIELD

◆ *Home of the Oneonta Tigers*
  (New York–Penn League, Single-A)

◆ *Location—95 River Street, Oneonta, New York*

◆ *Opened—1940*

◆ *Seating Capacity—4,200*

◆ *LF 333 CF 401 RF 335*

Among the ballplayers who played here are Don Mattingly, Al Leiter,
Bernie Williams, and Jorge Posada.

PATRICK COOGAN (Minor League Pitcher) "There's a huge difference coming from a college program like LSU, playing in front of eight thousand to ten thousand every night, coming into pro ball. Some Monday or Tuesday nights, you're playing in front of three hundred people, and two hundred are wives and friends. Facilities are considerably downsized compared to the SEC Conference. It makes for a humbling experience. But that's the trials that you have to go through in the minor leagues when you're trying to get to the big leagues. Learning humility, I think, is a big part of the experience."

MICKEY RIVERS (Former Major League Player) "My first year in the minor leagues [1969], I got to go to a city called [Twin Falls in] Magic Valley, Idaho. Minor league guys don't get paid as well. At that time, we got five dollars [a day], and we had to make it do. So some days you had to wash your undies, eat, and have to get back and forth to the ballpark. And we had to use the five bucks according to whether you wanted to eat that day or wash clothes that day. We had to walk home five to ten miles from the ballpark. We had one big place about seven guys stayed. It was a great experience—we learned how to cope."

Ira Rosen

SEAN DOUGLASS (Major League Pitcher) "When I first signed in 1997, I came to Rookie Ball. I was expecting nice fans, night games, nice baseball atmosphere. You work out at nine in the morning, it's boiling hot. Clubhouse has no air conditioning. Noon games, there's no fans, 100 degrees, 100 percent humidity, and the games take three, three and a half hours. After a couple of weeks you're saying to yourself, 'What did I get myself into?' As you move up, travel, the little things get easier. The game gets harder. The big thing is paying your dues—it's all worth it."

Dutchess Stadium

DUTCHESS STADIUM

◆ *Home of the Hudson Valley Renegades*
(New York–Penn League, Single-A)

◆ *Location—Route 9D, Fishkill, New York*

◆ *Opened—1994*

◆ *Seating Capacity—4,494*

◆ *LF 325 CF 400 RF 325*

Among the ballplayers who played here are Joe Kennedy, Toby Hall, and Travis Harper.

GARY PETTIS (Former Major League Player) "Going into professional baseball wasn't what everybody thought it was prior to arriving at their Rookie League field. Before we could take the infield, *we* had to drag the infield. Pick up rocks, bottles, whatever was lying on the ground."

Ira Rosen

MATT GALANTE (Major League Coach) "The year I managed in Newark, New York, in the New York–Penn League, the sun set in center field. We started the game with relief pitchers, because there was a point in the second or third inning when the sun went down and we had to stop the game for about forty minutes. After that, we'd bring in the starting pitchers."

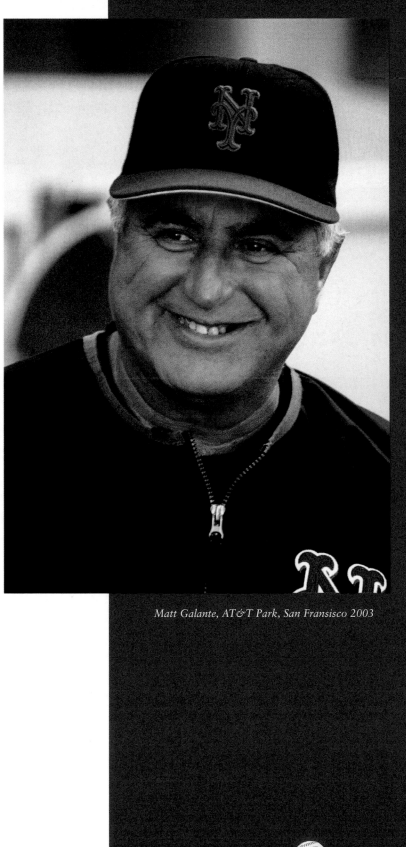

Matt Galante, AT&T Park, San Fransisco 2003

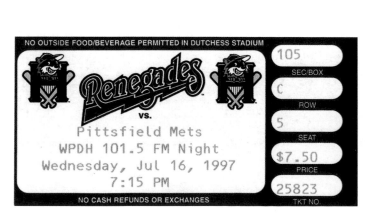

NO OUTSIDE FOOD/BEVERAGE PERMITTED IN DUTCHESS STADIUM

Renegades

vs.

Pittsfield Mets
WPDH 101.5 FM Night
Wednesday, Jul 16, 1997
7:15 PM

NO CASH REFUNDS OR EXCHANGES

105
SEC/BOX

C
ROW

5
SEAT

$7.50
PRICE

25823
TKT NO.

Edward LeLacheur Park

EDWARD A. LeLACHEUR PARK

- *Home of the Lowell Spinners
  (New York–Penn League, Single-A)*

- *Location—450 Aiken Street, Lowell, Massachusetts*

- *Opening Day—June 1998*

- *Seating Capacity—5,000*

- *LF 337 CF 400 RF 301*

Among the ballplayers who played here are Shea Hillenbrand and David Eckstein.

CASEY FOSSUM (Major League Pitcher) "My first home game with the Lowell Spinners. LeLacheur Park. Everybody was talking about how crazy it was at that place. They said they were going to do a wedding at the beginning of the game. Thirty minutes before the game, they made us get on the field and hold bats up, and two people actually got married on the field. We were witnesses and groomsmen."

JOANN WEBER (Minor League Executive) "Owning the Minor League team that we do [Lowell Spinners], I get to meet all the young players who come in. A lot of them come in here very frightened. It's their first time away from home for a lot of them. Some of them have been superstars all through T-ball, high school, college—they've always been on winning teams. Here, all of a

sudden they're not the star anymore. They're here with every other kid who's also the star. For some of these kids, especially the ones coming from the rural South, this is their first time in a big city [Boston], and the adjustment is very hard. Even though they may be 6'4" and weigh 250 pounds, they're kids underneath. I say, 'If you need to talk, come in.' When their parents are coming, I'll say, 'Oh, I have to meet your mom.' The ones who are slow and steady, who don't get crazy always wind up doing the best. Over the years our players have moved up. They write me, call me, e-mail me. These kids are nineteen, twenty, twenty-one—they need a little mothering."

Falcon Park

FALCON PARK

- *Home of the Auburn Doubledays*
  (New York–Penn League, Single-A)

- *Location—130 North Division Street, Auburn, New York*

- *Opened—June 1995*

- *Cost—$3.5 Million*

- *Seating Capacity—2,800*

- *LF 330 CF 400 RF 330*

Falcon Park is built on the site of the old Falcon Park, which was erected in 1927 and demolished in 1994. Among the ballplayers who played here are Luis Gonzalez, Roy Oswalt, and Kenny Lofton.

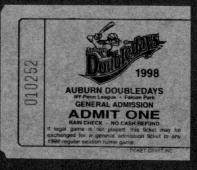

010252

Auburn Doubledays
1998
AUBURN DOUBLEDAYS
NY-Penn League · Falcon Park
GENERAL ADMISSION
ADMIT ONE
RAIN CHECK - NO CASH REFUND
If legal game is not played, this ticket may be exchanged for a general admission ticket to any 1998 regular season home game.
TICKET.CRAFT.INC

Ira Rosen

JIM KAAT (Former Major League Pitcher; Broadcaster) "My favorite year was 1958. I played for Missoula, Montana, in the Pioneer League. Jack McKeon was my playing manager. We had some great bus trips. Every now and then, the bus would get stopped by a rockslide. You didn't have cell phones in those days. You'd have to wait until the highway patrol or somebody showed up and cleared it off. We'd be outside playing catch, waiting for them.

Everything you did on the field, you got rewarded. My roommate was Sandy Valdespino—he was the leadoff hitter. For the first run scored, you got a pizza at Stockman's Pizza. If you had a ten-strikeout game, and I had quite a few of those, you got four or five banana splits at the Dairy Queen. For the first RBI, you got three dollars' worth of groceries, which we always gave to Chuck Weatherspoon—he was about the only guy on the team who was married."

Joseph L. Bruno Stadium

JOSEPH L. BRUNO STADIUM

- *Home of the Tri-City ValleyCats*
  (New York–Penn League, Single-A)

- *Location—Hudson Valley Community College, Troy, New York*

- *Opening Day—June 21, 2002*

- *Seating Capacity—4,500*

- *Cost—$13 Million*

- *LF 325 CF 400 RF 325*

Ira Rosen

IVAN DeJESUS (Former Major League Player; Minor League Manager) "It is not an easy job, an easy road to the big leagues. You've got to work hard, trust your talent. You need courage and intensity. At this level, it's too early to say if they're going to make it. They have tools. We have to develop them, year by year."

JARED GOTHREAUX (Minor League Player) "It's getting used to the same routine every day. This is the first stepping-stone. It's a job now, but it still has to be fun. If you don't, why do it? The biggest thing is, every hitter here is good. In college, there's always one or two in the lineup that are a little easier to get out. Here, the nine hole can hurt you just as bad as the four hole. You have to stay mentally strong, stay in shape, eat right . . . you really don't have that much time to eat."

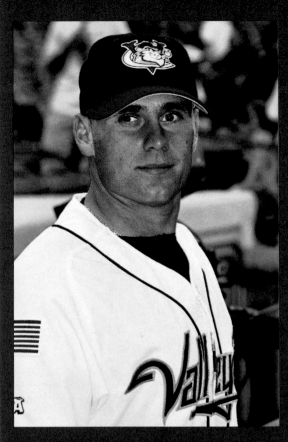

Jared Gothreaux, Tri-City ValleyCats, Joseph L. Bruno Stadium, 2002

Ivan DeJesus, Tri-City ValleyCats, Joseph L. Bruno Stadium, 2002

KeySpan Park

KEYSPAN PARK

- *Home of the Brooklyn Cyclones*
  (New York–Penn League, Single-A)

- *Location—1904 Surf Avenue, Brooklyn, New York*

- *Opening Day—June 25, 2001*

- *Cost—$39 million*

- *Seating Capacity—7,500*

- *LF 315 CF 412 RF 325*

Among the ballplayers who played here are Scott Kazmir and Brian Bannister.

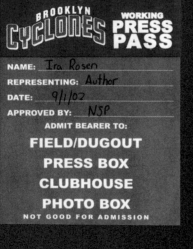

Ira Rosen

BLAKE WHEALY (Minor League Player) "Here in Brooklyn, we have kind of a unique situation in the minor leagues, where we get eight or nine thousand people at every game, and a lot of them are the same fans, diehards that come out 'cause they love baseball. A lot of them are young kids. From the time we get to the park and especially after we leave, there's always people looking for autographs. Whether they're collectors or just here for the first time—I've signed shirts, I've signed *faces*, all kinds of stuff. But autographs are a very cool thing, and the guys on the team do a great job of signing them. We get requests through the mail—there are three or four note cards in there—'Please sign these'—it's tough *not* to do. There's somebody, somewhere waiting for 'em."

Wes Carroll, Lakewood BlueClaws, FirstEnergy Park, 2002

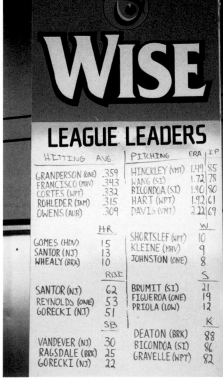

LEAGUE LEADERS

HITTING	AVG	PITCHING	ERA	IP
GRANDERSON (ONE)	.359	HINCKLEY (VMT)	1.49	85
FRANCISCO (MBV)	.343	WANG (SI)	1.72	78
CORTES (WPT)	.332	BICONDOA (SI)	1.90	80
ROHLEDER (TAM)	.315	HART (WPT)	1.92	61
OWENS (AUB)	.309	DAVIS (VMT)	2.22	69

HR			W
GOMES (HDV)	15	SHORTSLEF (WPT)	10
SANTOR (NJ)	13	KLEINE (MHV)	9
WHEALY (BRK)	10	JOHNSTON (ONE)	8

RBI			S
SANTOR (NJ)	62	BRUMIT (SI)	21
REYNOLDS (ONE)	53	FIGUEROA (ONE)	19
GORECKI (NJ)	51	PRIOLA (LOW)	12

SB			K
VANDEVER (NJ)	30	DEATON (BRK)	88
RAGSDALE (BRK)	25	BICONDOA (SI)	86
GORECKI (NJ)	22	GRAVELLE (WPT)	82

PART SIX

INDEPENDENT LEAGUES

Probably the best known of these non–Major League Baseball–affiliated leagues is the Northern League, founded—as was the Frontier League—in 1993. Consisting of twelve teams, it is part of a growing group of seven leagues (as of 2006). Others include the American Association, the Atlantic League, the Can-Am League, and the Golden League. The quality of play in these leagues varies depending on the team and who's pitching. The competition is roughly equal to Double-A in organized baseball. Some players here coming out of high school or college were overlooked by big-league clubs. Some are former affiliated team players looking to get back with a major league organization. The odds of making it from here to the Show in either case are long.

Skylands Park

SKYLANDS PARK

- *Current Home of the Sussex Skyhawks (Can-Am League, Independent)*

- *Former Home of the New Jersey Cardinals (New York–Penn League, Single-A)*

- *Location—County Road 565, Augusta, New Jersey*

- *Opened—June 1994*

- *Seating Capacity—4,336*

- *LF 330 CF 392 RF 330*

Among the ballplayers who played here are Matt Morris and Adam Kennedy.

PHIL PEPE (Author; Broadcaster) "For more than two decades I covered Major League Baseball as Yankees beat writer for the *New York Daily News*. In 1994, after leaving the newspaper, I began a new venture as the radio "voice" of the New Jersey Cardinals in the New York Penn League, and I felt as if I had been reborn. I experienced the same exhilaration, the same excitement, and the same anticipation I felt as a boy when I visited Ebbets Field in Brooklyn. I encountered young players with enthusiasm and joy for the game; young men who were eager, accessible and optimistic about their future."

BILL CAMPBELL (Former Major League Pitcher; Minor League Coach) "The good thing about having played in the big leagues and coming back to the minor leagues is helping the kids. Hopefully, you can instruct them, teach them enough . . . with their talent, help them get to the big leagues. Because that's the only place to play. It's the only place to coach or manage too . . . You have to work your way back up there.

Because of my delivery [as a pitcher], I'm a little more concerned with mechanics. I would never teach that to anybody. You try to keep it simple. If you see something that's going to be detrimental to the health of their arm, you have to mention it to them, try to get them out of it. Try to smooth them out to the point that it's taking as much strain off the arm as you can. There are certain mechanics that you have to do: balance, getting your hips turned, getting as much momentum towards your target as possible. Most of the kids here have been very receptive, have tried some things. At this level, you're trying to get them to establish the fastball, working the changeup. They have a tendency to come out of college, because of the aluminum bats, to "trick" a lot. So you want to get them to use more fastballs. Some of these pitchers down here, they get a little too much movement in their delivery. So I tell them, 'pick a guy who's got your body type maybe throws similar to you and watch him pitch.'"

KEN HARRELSON (Former Major League Player; Broadcaster) "My first stop was Olean, New York, in the New York–Penn League. We got $1.75 a day meal money and plenty to eat."

Bill Campbell, New Jersey Cardinals,
KeySpan Park, 2002

Yale Field

YALE FIELD

- *Home of the New Haven County Cutters*
  (Can-Am League, Independent)

- *Location—252 Derby Avenue, West Haven, Connecticut*

- *Year Built—1927; First Game—1928*

- *Opening Day (after renovation)—April 14, 1994*

- *Seating Capacity—6,200*

- *LF 330 CF 405 RF 315*

Former home of the New Haven Ravens, 1994–2003 (Eastern League, Double-A). Among the ballplayers who played here are Todd Helton, Joe Cronin, and Ron Darling.

WILTON VERAS (Former Major League Player) "Sometimes it looks like you're having fun, but it's tough for us because we have long trips, long games. How we play the game—we just try to have fun."

GAVIN OSTEEN (Former Minor League Pitcher) "I've been playing for thirteen years. My first five or six years were tough. There wasn't any money in the game at that stage. When you're in the minor leagues, in the off-season you have to find a job. Plus, you have to stay in shape. If you're a major leaguer, you don't have to go to work [in the off-season]. It takes a toll to work and try to prepare for the next season. When I became a six-year free agent, then I

Ira Rosen

started making money where I could live. I'm a career minor leaguer. I've gotten called up, and I've been sent right back without even throwing a pitch. You hit the crossroads where you get a little old, and now I'm in independent ball and we make nothing. You can't even count on this to pay the bills. Now it's time to start thinking about finding a job elsewhere, doing something else. I've tried to get overseas to make some money to get out of the game. If I could get a Triple-A job, that would be great also. I still think I can pitch. I've proven it year after year, that I've been successful. I'm just not ready to quit. I'm close. Very close."

JASON RYAN (Former Major League Pitcher) "The main thing is to keep yourself in shape mentally and physically. It's a grueling job. You don't get a lot of off days. A lot of us in the independent leagues are coming off surgeries. Thank God for this league, or a lot of us wouldn't have jobs."

Jason Ryan, Camden Riversharks,
Campbell's Field, 2002

Campbell's Field

CAMPBELL'S FIELD

- *Home of the Camden Riversharks*
  (Atlantic League, Independent)
- *Location—401 North Delaware Avenue, Camden, New Jersey*
- *Opening Day—May 11, 2001*
- *Cost—$20.5 million*
- *Seating Capacity—6,425*
- *LF 325 CF 405 RF 325*

Campbell's Field is situated on the Delaware River, with the Ben Franklin Bridge and the Philadelphia skyline in the background.

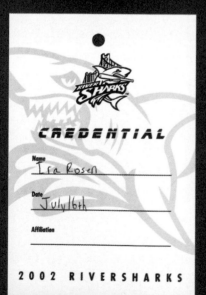

CREDENTIAL

Name
Ira Rosen

Date
July 16th

Affiliation

2002 RIVERSHARKS

158 Ira Rosen

KASH BEAUCHAMP (Minor League Manager) "At the time, I was six feet, one inch tall, had a little pop in my bat. Had a very good minor league career, played for fourteen years. I think the biggest disappointment, and I found this out after the season, when Pat Gillick called my father and told him what happened: I was in Toledo and there was a collision at home plate. I fractured my scapula and missed the rest of that year. I was going to get called up the next day to the big leagues. If I had known that, I probably wouldn't have run the catcher over. It was a tough break . . . it wasn't meant to be. I played five years in Triple-A."

WILL PENNYFEATHER (Former Major League Player) "It's tough, especially here in the Independent League. We have to work an off-season job to make

enough money to make it through the season. You keep playing hopefully to get that big payday. I'm looking to get overseas, Japan or Korea, trying to feed the family."

JOHN BRISCOE (Former Major League Pitcher) "The minor leagues, it's more of a game. The big leagues is almost like a show. You don't see the grind as much. You're in a beautiful ballpark every day, in a big city, making a lot of money. There are a lot of distractions. Down here, there are not that many distractions. I've kind of come to grips with fact that I probably won't ever get back there. But I just love playing."

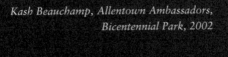

Kash Beauchamp, Allentown Ambassadors,
Bicentennial Park, 2002

Commerce Bank Ballpark

COMMERCE BANK BALLPARK

- *Home of the Somerset Patriots
  (Atlantic League, Independent)*

- *Location—1 Patriots Park, Bridgewater, New Jersey*

- *Opening Day—June 7, 1999*

- *Cost—$17.7 million*

- *Seating Capacity—6,100*

- *LF 317 CF 402 RF 315*

Among the ballplayers who played here are Tim Raines Jr. and Jerome Walton.

TOM O'MALLEY (Former Major League Player; Minor League Manager) "There's a lot of responsibility that comes with the job. It's not just being a manager and making moves throughout a game. It's making sure the equipment is there, making sure we've got enough balls for the game. There are so many different roles that you have to partake in. It's not easy in the minor leagues. [In] the major leagues there's so many people to take part and everyone has a particular role. Minor leagues, anything can happen at any time."

DARRIN WINSTON (Former Major League Pitcher) "I was kind of caught between old school baseball and the way that things are run now. I've played

Ira Rosen

fourteen years; I've been fortunate to have played that long. I've got a great family, my five kids are with me. [My wife has] been with me since day one.

"When they say, 'Baseball is life,' for us, we knew nothing else. We had children in Rookie Ball, which was an oddity. We chased after that dream. Deep down, I still believe I have the talent. I was young once, was healthy and strong. At that time, it wasn't, 'Let's bring up young guys.' It was, 'Let's go with veterans.' Now I'm a veteran, and these kids get rushed to the big leagues. We had to learn at Double-A, Triple-A."

Darrin Winston, Somerset Patriots,
Commerce Bank Ballpark, 2002

Bears & Eagles Riverfront Stadium

BEARS AND EAGLES RIVERFRONT STADIUM

- *Home of the Newark Bears*
  (Atlantic League, Independent)

- *Location—450 Broad Street, Newark, New Jersey*

- *Opening Day—July 16, 1999*

- *Cost—$30 million*

- *Seating Capacity—6,200*

- *LF 302 CF 394 RF 323*

Among the ballplayers who played here are Jose Canseco, Jim Leyritz, and Jaime Navarro.

AARON LEDESMA (Former Major League Player) "Being in the minor leagues makes you appreciate the time you spent in the big leagues. You take a lot of things for granted [in the big leagues], like the hotels, flying. Now that I'm back in independent ball . . . if I get back to the big leagues, I'm going to appreciate every minute. The game doesn't change at all; it's the same game

Ira Rosen

here as it is up there. As a matter of fact, I think it's a little bit easier up there. Because of the lights there's no bad hops; the traveling—it just makes everything a lot easier up there."

SPARKY LYLE (Former Major League Pitcher; Minor League Manager) "It's one of the most pure forms of baseball, with us being independent. The guys don't make a lot of money—they're here to try and get back to organizations, which is something that we try to do for them. I enjoy the pureness of it, I guess. They're here to better their skills. They're definitely not here for the money; they barely make a living. They try to get to Korea, Japan, whatever from here. It's a learning experience for some, and for some, maybe it's the end of the line."

LOU COLLIER (Major League Player) "A lot of guys get to the major leagues and think they have to do something different. They call you up because they know what you can do, and they just want you to do that. Down here, small crowds, games drag on, you have to try to stay focused."

Lou Collier, Scranton/Wilkes-Barre Red Barons, Lackawanna County Stadium, 2004

Yogi Berra Stadium

YOGI BERRA STADIUM

- *Home of the New Jersey Jackals (Can-Am League, Independent)*
- *Location—Montclair State University, Little Falls, New Jersey*
- *Opening Day—June 5, 1998*
- *Cost—$13 million*
- *Seating Capacity—3,748*
- *LF 308 CF 398 RF 308*

Among the ballplayers who played here are Mark Lemke and Pete Rose Jr.

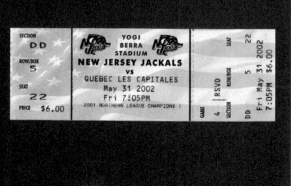

  Ira Rosen

ERIC CAMMACK (Former Major League Pitcher) "I was ready to go home after the first week and a half. We ended up winning the whole thing. What are the odds, my first year in pro ball? Next year in St. Lucie, that was when I really started to throw well. My first big-league camp in 2000, I knew I wasn't going to make the team. When you get out there, you realize, 'These guys don't have anything that I don't have except they're just more consistent.' And that's the whole thing. My first day in the big leagues, Matt Franco goes, 'Hey, E, how many days you got in the big leagues now?' I said, 'One.' He goes, 'That's one more than a lot of guys will ever get.' "

Eric Cammack, Binghamton Mets,
NYSEG Stadium, 2002